WEATHER LANGUAGE

WEATHER LANGUAGE

by Julius Fast

Wyden Books

Manufactured in the United States of America.

FIRST EDITION

Trade distribution by Simon and Schuster
A Division of Gulf + Western Corporation
New York, New York 10020

Designed by Tere LoPrete

Library of Congress Cataloging in Publication Data

Fast, Julius, 1918-
    Weather language.
    Bibliography: p.
    1. Weather—Mental and physiological effects.
2. Climatology, Medical. I. Title.
QP82.2.C5F37   613.1'1   78-21291
ISBN 0-88326-157-X

For my sister-in-law, Dorothy

Contents

Contents

Contents

WEATHER LANGUAGE

Chapter One

How Weather Works

My uncle Jim, a successful farmer, subscribed to all the available planting guides. He had a great crop record, but once, in a confiding moment, he told me, "These guides all use some pretty fancy apparatus to forecast the weather, but I don't pay much attention to what they say."

"Then how do you figure out when to plant?" I asked.

He looked at me speculatively for a moment, as if wondering whether I'd believe him. Then, glancing up at the sky, he said, "It's in my bones. I know when the weather's going to change. And I know when a frost is due."

"But how? How do you know?"

"There's a pain I feel, the worst kind of misery. My whole body tells me a cold snap's coming. It says, 'Don't plant yet!'"

The weather language my uncle's body spoke is part of man's oldest knowledge, yet it has always been relegated to folklore and old wives' tales. *When my big toe aches, it's going to rain. You mustn't exert yourself in hot weather. If you wear rubbers indoors, you'll hurt your eyes. Sleep with closed windows because the night air is harmful. Sleep with open windows for fresh air. Cold air can give you hives. Sunspots cause cancer.*

Some of these tales are true, some are nonsense, but yesterday's nonsense may become tomorrow's truth. I was brought up to believe it healthy to sleep with open windows; now research is beginning to confirm the old-fashioned view that open windows at night are unhealthy. The research deserves respect because, for the first time, a body of scientific knowledge is becoming available that makes it possible to apply logic to much of the old folklore about the weather.

In the late 1950s, a group of international scientists got together to form a new society, an organization devoted to exploring the link between weather and physical as well as emotional health. They named their group the International Society of Biometeorologists. It recognized that the weather has profound effects on human beings, and set out to explore that impact and study the surprisingly numerous ways of overcoming its dangers and discomforts.

Although, like my uncle Jim, most people agree that weather affects us, whether we're healthy or sick, very few doctors consider the weather seriously when they treat a patient. They may give strict orders about diet and medication, recommend exercise or limit activity, but very rarely do they consider the weather in their instructions. At least this is true in the United States up to this writing. In Europe, as we shall see, doctors are more receptive and advanced in this field.

In researching this book, I found that the library of the Academy of Medicine in New York City had no copies of the *International Journal of Biometeorology*. The library at the Museum of Natural History had a few back issues. Only the Science and Technology Department of the New York Public Library contained all the back numbers. The message is clear: the new science is still of greatest concern to nonmedical researchers.

In 1975, however, there were four physicians on the nine-member executive board of the International Society of Biometeorology. One was from the United States, the others from Poland, Italy, and Switzerland. Of the other members, three were physiologists, from Germany, Japan, and the United States. One member was a geophysicist from the Netherlands and one a veterinary and medical entomologist from Canada.

While medical professionals in the United States may be slow in recognizing the new science because they are too conventional to accept its theories or too busy to become involved, the best definition of biometeorology is to be found not in Webster's but in another American work—Dorland's *Medical Dictionary*: "that branch of ecology that deals with the effects on living organisms of the extraorganic aspects of the physical environment such as temperature, humidity, barometric pressure, rate of air flow and air ionization."

This is not only an accurate definition of biometeorology; it's also a concise definition of weather. We could paraphrase the definition as "the way in which weather affects life." In our case, human life.

What Is a Weather Sensitive?

Biometeorology, a fascinating science, is more than a scientific curiosity. It is of great help to many of us, and of some help to all.

For many years I was plagued with mild migraine headaches that often interfered with my work. I went from internist to ophthalmologist to neurologist; I even tried a chiropractor. No one could find an organic reason for my problem.

In desperation, I started keeping a chart, trying to find some connection between my headaches and what I was doing, what I had eaten, how much I used my eyes, what stress I had been under—but nothing seemed to add up.

Finally a friend, a fellow migraine sufferer from the West

Coast, suggested I get in touch with Dr. Lee Kudrow, director of the California Medical Clinic for Headache in Encino. After listening to my problem, Dr. Kudrow asked me if I had considered the weather. "We've found that the weather has a profound effect on migraine headaches," he told me.

"What kind of weather?" I asked.

"Well—prestorm conditions, barometric changes, even winds like our Santa Ana. Many of these weather conditions create an excess of positive ions that can alter the cerebral serotonin levels and bring on vascular migraine headaches. Try matching your chart against the weather."

I didn't understand all his terminology, but I took his advice and found, to my surprise, that the one event that always followed my headaches was a storm. Let the weather go from good to bad and I was off, my head pounding like crazy. I realized then that I was *weather sensitive*.

From that point on I became an avid late-news weather-watcher on TV. At the first announcement of a coming storm I head for the medicine cabinet—and so far so good! Making that connection between a storm and my headache allowed me to manage my migraines. They're mild, and if I catch them in time a few APC tablets will take care of them.

Migraine headaches are only one small tip of the bio-meteorological iceberg. There is a long and startling list of symptoms that changing weather can cause in healthy people, and in sick ones.

Millions of people in America are, like myself, weather sensitives. Some react with headaches, but there are over two dozen other symptoms that can turn up with every turn in the weather. Later in this book I'll show you an exact way of determining your own degree of weather sensitivity, and the type of weather you are sensitive to.

Biometeorologists estimate that one out of every three

people is extremely weather sensitive. Others see weather sensitivity as a spectrum. They believe that everyone, young and old, male and female, is to some degree affected physically and emotionally by the weather. At one end of the spectrum are those who react strongly, and at the other end the few who feel very little when the weather acts up.

The vast majority of the population falls between these extremes. They are weather sensitive to one degree or another. When the weather changes, they are troubled. Their trouble can be as slight as a vague feeling of uneasiness, or it can range from migraine headaches through severe depression, sleepless nights, back pain, stomach upsets, loss of appetite, irritability, and lack of judgment—the list goes on and even includes accidents and an inability to work efficiently.

Of course, any one of these symptoms may be due to other causes, but they *can* be due to the weather, and for people who are extremely weather sensitive, weather is the prime factor.

Most people are not aware that the weather is to blame when they manifest these symptoms. It's hard to realize how much of an impact weather can have on your physical and mental health. But once you discover how weather sensitive you are, you can begin to take steps to cope with your sensitivity. You can learn how to protect your health and increase your productivity, how to overcome that puzzling depression or that unusual restlessness, that loss of appetite, those vague pains, aches, and general fatigue that make you hate to get out of bed.

All these and many more troubles can be a direct effect of weather changes, of barometric highs and lows, passing fronts, heat, cold, humidity, even thunderstorms.

This book will help you discover just how weather sensitive you are; how to read the hidden messages your body sends you;

Learning what the weather can do to your body and emo-
and how to relate them to the changing weather around you.
tions is the first step toward coping with weather sensitivity

and functioning at your full potential. Understanding the weather sensitivity of others can help you on the job, in your love life, and with your own family.

Weather sensitivity is one result of weather changes, but there are other, more startling results. Did you know that admissions to mental hospitals increase with certain weather patterns? That other patterns cause an increase in cancer deaths? That accidents at home, at work, and on the highways are more numerous with one type of weather change, while another type will depress your score on an IQ test?

Fortunately, once you understand the intricate connection between weather and your life, you *can* do something about it. What you need is a warning system to alert you to the potential danger to your health when the weather changes.

This book can be your system. Even simpler would be a program of TV and radio coverage of the weather that included its impact on your health. It would not only tell you what the weather is and is going to be, but also how such a change may affect your body and mind.

Healthy, weather-sensitive people would benefit from this; anyone with a serious illness such as heart disease, asthma, or emphysema might find it a lifesaver. They run a real and serious risk when certain weather patterns produce just that extra amount of stress necessary to kill a person weakened by one of these illnesses.

Out of Eden

To understand the effect of weather on people and what we can do about it, we must understand some basic facts about weather. We have always been at the mercy of the weather. A human being is a fragile, vulnerable creature, and must keep body temperature very close to 98.6° Fahrenheit. Without clothing or shelter, humans cannot survive naked for long in extremely cold or hot climates.

The real secret of Adam's and Eve's nakedness was probably that Eden, in addition to its innocence, must have enjoyed a temperate climate. Even after that awkward mixup with the apple, the two were able to make do with fig leaves. But fig leaves are small protection against the cold. Once they were expelled from the garden, our antecedents needed something more substantial. They were forced to invent clothes.

He may have lost Eden, but the rest of Adam's life on earth, and his children's lives, took on new dimensions after he found that magic trio—clothes, fire, and shelter

Mankind's first victory in its fight against the weather was the discovery of shelter, but shelter wasn't enough. Mankind had also to gain control of its own food supply by mastering the art of domesticating animals and learning to plant grain. For these skills it needed more room, and so it added another innovation—migration. People began to spread out in all directions.

These migrations took them to lands with varied and changeable weather. In some, the seasons alternated between very hot and very cold. To survive, humanity had to step up its never-ending struggle against the weather. Even when the weather was at its best, people knew that change would soon occur, and they had to prepare for that change.

One certainty about the weather, they discovered, is that it would always be around. They could ignore it or enjoy it, fight it or surrender to it—but it wouldn't go away. Another sure thing was that no matter what the weather was, they knew it would change.

It is this element of change that has fascinated human beings from primitive times to now. Our ancestors watched the behavior of animals, the length of their pelts, the way the trees grew, the way the sky looked, the shape of the clouds, and the angle of the sun to predict heat and cold, rain, and shine.

They had to know the weather in order to know when to sow and reap, when to shelter their animals and when to graze them. Weather was a basic part of their lives, and those who had a weather curiosity strong enough to devise even the most rudimentary methods of forecasting had an edge on survival.

Today, to get an accurate weather forecast, we use sophisticated modern instruments—satellites, weather balloons, computers, and radar, as well as the older thermometers, and hygrometers—but the basic reason behind our need to know the weather is no longer stark survival. We can get along reasonably well in almost any weather. We do welcome the scientists who forecast the weather and we are interested in what they say, for all of us are interested in protecting ourselves against the impact of the weather.

It's possible that some of that interest is programmed into our genes. It is so insistent because evolution favored the survival of the weather-curious, and we are all the products of evolution.

What Makes the Weather?

What is the weather that it should so fascinate us? What makes it change?

Four basic elements create weather. The first is out of this world—about 93 million miles out of it! Our sun. That seemingly eternal hydrogen furnace, in spite of its distance, is absolutely necessary for weather and life.

The second element in the creation of weather is the sphere we live on, the earth and its overall shape.

The third is the more intimate structures of that sphere, its oceans, valleys, mountains, deserts, ice caps, lakes, and rivers.

The fourth element is the casing of gas around the sphere, which seals it off from outer space. The casing? Our atmosphere.

Let's consider each. The sun is a monstrous furnace that

burns hydrogen and spits electromagnetic energy into space in an indiscriminate, incredibly wasteful fashion. Only one two-billionth of all this energy hits the earth, but in one minute we receive more energy from the sun than we use in a year.

The energy of sunlight comes to us in a rainbow spectrum from invisible ultraviolet to invisible infrared. In between are all the visible rays of light.

The heat of the sun is absorbed by the earth and then radiated back towards space. But a change in wavelength that it undergoes in its absorption prevents it from escaping. Some is trapped by the gases in the atmosphere, and some by the water vapor in the atmosphere. This heat, caught from the sun and discharged into the air, causes the air to move, to become breezes, winds, hurricanes, and typhoons, and it also causes the lightning, rain, and snow.

The earth itself, that spinning, slightly flattened sphere that swings around the sun in a long ellipse, is also responsible for much of its own weather. Its rotation also causes the wind to blow and the ocean to flow. Its rounded shape permits some parts of it to receive more sunlight than others, while its tilt on its axis causes the change of seasons.

The wrinkled contour of the earth has still another effect on weather. Mountain ranges channel the winds, block water vapor from one area and pour it down as rain on another, shut out cold winds, and cause rivers and streams to flow. The bodies of water on the earth hold heat and warm some climates while they cool others. They release water vapor into the air, and in the polar regions they keep the land locked in a permanent freeze.

The fourth element that makes weather is the atmosphere, that blanket of air that swaddles the earth, protecting it and insulating it from the cold of outer space. Without air above us the sun would raise our daytime temperature to 180°, too high for life, while at night the earth's surface would fall to 200° below zero!

Among other things, the weight of all this air has an effect on weather. At sea level the atmosphere weighs nearly 15 pounds per square inch. At 18,000 feet it weighs half that. The air carries water and carbon dioxide, two substances involved in weather. These are the basic elements that cause the changes in the weather. Their interplay and reaction on each other in an almost infinite series of permutations and combinations makes it surprising not that weather changes, but that we ever experience the same weather twice.

How Hot Is Heat?

We talk of weather very glibly nowadays, but before the ubiquitous TV weatherpersons took over, weather, to most of us, meant rain or shine, hot or cold. We know vaguely that there are things called highs and lows, fronts and occlusions, depressions and isobars, but still, when all the weather maps are carefully explained, what we still want to know is, "Will it rain tomorrow or not?" And after that, "How hot or cold will it be?" Thanks to biometeorology, we can now ask many more questions and get many more answers.

We cannot understand the weather's full impact on our body systems until we know something about the factors that make up the weather—the most obvious being temperature.

We measure the heat of the air with a thermometer, and the most common kinds have bulbs with either red-dyed alcohol or silvery mercury. When the thermometer is heated, the mercury or alcohol expands and moves up a calibrated scale. The height of the column tells us just how hot it is.

Weather forecasters enclose the thermometer in a box with louvers for air circulation. This shields it from the sun's radiation, but allows it to measure the heat in the air.

The calibrated scale on the thermometer is measured in either Celsius or Fahrenheit. The Fahrenheit scale is rather clumsy, with freezing set at 32° and boiling at 212°, but it's the scale we're all familiar with in the United States, although that is beginning to change as Celsius is introduced as part of the shift to metric measurements. The Celsius scale is more logical. It puts freezing at 0° and boiling at 100° and divides the space between into an even hundred degrees.

There is usually a difference in temperature between the air and the ground. Air temperature fluctuates whereas ground temperature is steadier. Dig deep enough into the earth and you will find a constant temperature the year round. When the air temperature is above freezing, and the temperature near the ground is below freezing, we speak of a *ground frost*. We call it an *air frost* when the air temperature is below freezing.

It is interesting, considering the difficulty most of us have in living through ordinary summer heat, to know that some people have survived temperatures of over 122° Fahrenheit and that some desert dwellers regularly endure heat of over 104°. The average summer temperature in New York City is a few degrees over 68, in London a few degrees below. In winter the average in New York is 23°, whereas in Moscow 14° is common. A good Siberian winter will drop to −58°. The lowest temperature ever recorded was in Antarctica: −129°F.

These are all Fahrenheit temperatures, and I use the Fahrenheit scale all through this book. In weather reports, the Celsius scale, devised by Anders Celsius, a Swedish astronomer, is given as well, but the Celsius scale is not as familiar to most of us in the United States.

How to Measure Air Pressure

Around the middle of the seventeenth century, an Italian scientist, Evangelista Torricelli, took a long glass tube, closed at one end, and filled it with mercury. He then stood the open end in a bowl of mercury. A column of mercury 30 inches high remained in the glass tube.

This proved, Torricelli decided, that something was pressing down so hard on the surface of the bowl of mercury that it forced the mercury up inside the tube. Only one thing could push down with such force—the vast blanket of air that covers the world.

The entire blanket weighs at least 5,600 trillion tons, but the Torricelli tube is only an inch in diameter, and the pressure on that is from a one-inch column of air extending up to the farthest reaches of the atmosphere—and that weighs nearly 15 pounds, enough to force the mercury up 30 inches.

It doesn't seem like a great deal, but every human being carries an atmospheric weight on his or her body ranging from 10 to 20 tons, depending on size and skin area. Fortunately, the same pressure exists inside us pressing out, and it also exists inside every cell of our bodies or we'd all be squashed flat at once.

In some sealed-off portions of the body, changes in that pressure cannot be equalized, and changes in the pressure of the air occur continuously. These sealed-off areas, our joints for example, may become very painful when the air pressure goes up or down.

Even today, some three hundred years after Torricelli discovered it, we use a simple variation of his closed tube to measure air pressure. We call it a barometer. There are other types of barometers that take the form of collapsible boxes with most of the air pumped out. Like our joints, these boxes are sensitive to pressure changes and expand or contract accordingly.

We measure heat in degrees, Fahrenheit or Celsius, and we measure pressure in *millibars*. The term comes from millimeters of mercury read from the barometer, 1 millibar being equal to 1.02 grams per square centimeter. The average pressure of the atmosphere at sea level is about 1,000 millibars. From 920 to 1,060 millibars is the usual range of pressure fluctuation, even in severe storms.

It's Not the Heat, It's the Humidity

The mantle of air that wraps the earth is a mixture of gases, including the life-giving oxygen and a great deal of water in the form of invisible vapor. The amount of water in the air, the *humidity,* varies tremendously. The warmer the air, the more water it can hold—up to a point. This is the saturation point. After that the air gets rid of its water as rain, snow, hail, or fog.

We measure the amount of water in the air in terms of *relative humidity.* Fully saturated air at 50° Fahrenheit has a relative humidity of 100 percent. That means that every cubic meter of air contains 9.4 grams of water. If a cubic meter of air has half this amount, the relative humidity is 50 percent. A general rule of thumb: the higher the humidity, the worse you feel. Since warm air can hold more water than cold, it's easy to understand the old complaint, "It's not the heat, it's the humidity!"

Some Ill Winds That Blow No Good

The great moisture-laden covering of air that presses down on our world is rarely still. It blows hot and cold, fast and slow, sometimes from one direction, sometimes from another. We label winds according to their direction and how far, in degrees, they are blowing from the compass point, N-40 (forty miles per hour from the north) or S-20 (twenty miles per hour from the south). But folklore preferred more intimate names—Mother West Wind, Jack Frost's North Wind, howlers and zephyrs and the Sweet South Wind.

The speed of the wind is a second descriptive label, and we usually give this in miles per hour. A scale devised in the nineteenth century by a British admiral, Sir Francis Beaufort, describes winds in terms of the damage they do on a scale of 0 to 12, with 0 a perfect calm where smoke rises vertically. Four on the Beaufort scale raises dust and loose paper and stirs small branches. Number 8 breaks the twigs of trees and impedes the progress of cars, while number 12, at 64 to 72 miles per hour, does widespread damage. The twelve-point scale has subsequently been enlarged to seventeen in order to include devastating winds of hurricane force.

Winds increase our sense of cold. The *wind-chill factor* derives from the fact that, the temperature remaining constant, the stronger the wind, the colder we feel. We can tolerate cold weather, but combine it with a wind and we're in trouble!

The wrinkled surface of the earth directs and characterizes the winds. Winds will race down the troughs between mountains, but move more slowly at ground level because of friction. They may be filled with moisture when they blow in from the ocean, or be hot and dry when they come from the desert.

The foehn is a much-dreaded European wind from the northern Alps. This hot, dry mountain wind causes all sorts of depressions and mental upsets. It comes into being when a wind, heavy with water, meets a mountain range and blows up the mountain. As the wind gets higher, it gets colder and its water condenses out as rain. Over the crest of the mountain, the wind, dry now, becomes a foehn as it picks up heat from the friction of its passage down the other side of the mountain.

The chinook in North America is the same sort of uncomfortable wind and so is the Andean zonda. The mistral is a cold and bitter ill wind that blows through the Rhone Valley in France, unhealthy in reputation and fact.

Some winds are so violent that they can rip up entire cities. Hurricanes that form in the Caribbean often devastate our Gulf and East coasts. Hurricanes are violent winds that whirl as they tear along. In the center there is an area of calm, the eye. When this passes over, the sun may shine for a moment or two, then the wind and rain pound in ferociously from the other direction. In the Northern Hemisphere, the hurricane spins counterclockwise—in the Southern Hemisphere, clockwise.

These violent winds carry different names in different lands. We call it a hurricane when it forms in the Caribbean. In the China Sea, the same wind is a typhoon. The ones that blow from the Indian Ocean and the Bay of Bengal are called cyclones.* The hurricane is said by most authorities to take its name from Huracán, the West Indian god of storms, but by any name it is still a wild and deadly wind.

There are also winds called anticyclones that rotate around a high-pressure eye instead of the cyclone's (or hurricane's) low-pressure one. Anticyclones are mild winds and cause dry, unsettled weather. When one forms in the winter in America, it is cold and unpleasant, but those that form in the summer are usually clear and hot. In Europe, anticyclones bring mild weather. They blow in the opposite direction from cyclones— clockwise in the Northern Hemisphere and counterclockwise in the Southern.

The most terrible and violent winds of all are tornadoes. A friend of mine at the University of Kansas in Lawrence told me of a tornado she experienced. "It was midday, but suddenly everything was quiet, deadly quiet. Not a leaf stirred. Then the sky darkened to an ominous, terrible green, and then the sound hit us, a shock wave of it, and we could see the funnel of the tornado racing across the cornfields, swaying from side to side!

"I saw houses ripped open, fences torn up, and an automobile lifted like a matchstick. There was no place we could go, no place to hide. We just stood there, stunned, and it was the barest luck that it turned aside less than a mile from us."

Tornadoes like this can roar along at shattering speeds, sometimes at over 300 miles an hour. As a rule they occur in

* There is an unfortunate ambiguity in weather terminology. *Cyclone* can mean both a hurricane (in Bengal) or any counterclockwise-rotating low-pressure center.

our Midwest, and their exact origin is still unknown. When they occur over water, they are milder and suck up the water to form waterspouts.

What Are Fronts, Depressions, and Occlusions?

For years I used to sit in front of my TV set each evening and listen to weatherpeople talk of warm fronts stretching across the Eastern seaboard and cold fronts coming down from Canada, while occlusions and depressions sat over this state or that. I listened, but I was never quite sure of what a front was. On the map it seemed a series of V's connected by a line, but I had never seen a line like that in nature. When I finally found out what a front was, I felt cheated. It was so simple, after all!

Although the blanket of air around the earth serves to even out the heat of the sun, its own heat is very uneven. It's made up of masses of air, some cold, some hot. Such a mass is pretty much the same temperature inside itself, but, as it moves along, the leading edge, or *front*, of it causes some intense weather changes, clouds, and rain.

When air masses of different temperatures meet head on, the boundary between them is the front. When a mass of warm air moves into a mass of cold air, the boundary is called a *warm* front. When cold air moves into warm, the boundary is a *cold* front. It's as simple as that.

Since warm air is lighter than cold—after all, hot air makes balloons go up—and warm air has more moisture than cold, when a warm air mass meets a cold one, the warm one rises over the cold one, and its moisture condenses out in heavy clouds or rain.

Fronts may be hundreds of miles long, and they slip sideways as they move. Of course you cannot see the lines of the weather map in nature, but you can usually spot a warm front moving into a cold air mass by the cloud formations marking its boundary. These start as feathery wisps of cirrus cloud. As the warm front moves in, the clouds lower and thicken and become cumulus, then rain clouds. After the front has passed, the sun breaks through and the weather is warm and pleasant.

A cold front, moving forward into warm air, comes on very quickly, digging under the warmer air and lifting it up like a big scoop. The weather change may then be much more violent, with ominous clouds, thunderstorms, and heavy rainfall. But once the front passes, the air is cold and clear.

When the air pressure between cold front and warm front is low, or depressed, the wind circles and the weather gets stormy and wet. In the United States such *depressions* usually move from west to east and the fronts alternate, first cold, then warm, then cold again.

When the trailing cold front overtakes the warm front in a depression, we get an *occlusion*. The weather accompanying the occlusion is a troubling mix of warm and cold, heavy clouds, rain, clearing, and then more rain.

The Electricity Around Us

Only a small portion of the energy emitted by the sun reaches the earth, but this is still enough to warm our planet. The blanket of air around us traps the heat of the sun and lets less escape than comes in.

The moon, lacking a protective atmosphere to hold heat, can get extremely hot when the sun shines on its surface, and bitterly cold when there is no sun. Venus, on the other hand, has a cloud cover much thicker than earth's and so holds a tremendous amount of the sun's heat, enough to make its surface a boiling desert.

Striking a happy medium, at least for the existence of life, the earth never cools down too much, nor heats up too much.

In our atmosphere, clouds of water vapor and dust absorb a great deal of the sun's radiation, so that what filters down to the surface is neither deadly nor harmful.

We're familiar with all the visible radiation of the sun, the white light that we see during the day, but the sun also sends out invisible radiation—gamma rays, X rays, and ultraviolet light above the visible spectrum and infrared rays, microwaves, and radio waves below it. Unfortunately, the sun doesn't radiate energy at a regular rate. Sunspots and solar flares erratically throw out random bursts of extra energy. We know only that this extra energy disrupts our communications systems; otherwise we know there is a definite connection between it and health.

Most of us are not aware of all this extra energy, but some people can almost anticipate energy disturbances, whether from the sun or from the skies. When I was a boy, I had a neighbor, Johann, a man in his sixties who used to keep us entranced with wild, slightly off-color stories. We never told our parents about Johann's stories for fear they would end, but Johann had one trick that was never hidden from children or grown-ups. He could predict a thunderstorm and tell us just how much lightning would come with it. And he was rarely wrong.

I always thought that Johann's accuracy was just luck until I found out that when a bolt of lightning passes through the atmosphere it generates a great deal of heat along with negative and positive ionization of the air and electromagnetic impulses.

Like Johann, some people are sensitive to these electrical effects. Since the charges travel much faster than the changing weather, electrically sensitive people can feel the storm approaching long before it arrives. That's how they earn reputations as weather sages.

Lightning forms negative and positive *ions* in the air, and so do a great many other changing weather conditions. Ions are formed when energy—light, radiation, electricty—hits a molecule of gas. An electron in the outermost ring circling the nucleus is knocked off; such a molecule is called positive. The wayward electron then attaches itself to another molecule, which is called negative.

When the number of electrons equals the number of protons in the nucleus of an atom, it is neutral. One electron too many makes it negative; one too few makes it positive.

Radioactivity from the earth can create different ions, and so can radiation from the sun. Dust storms can create them too, through the friction of the particles of dust, and so can the friction of ice crystals in snowfalls and the friction of falling water in rain. When it rains on land, 75 percent of the rain is usually ion-positive. Thunderstorms tend to produce negative ions.

In addition to charged ions, storms emit extralong electromagnetic waves. These waves are called *sferics* (from atmospherics). Not only do they have an effect on health, but their unique penetrating power enables them to reach all the way inside our homes.

Electromagnetic fields exist because of the different electromagnetic potential between the ground and the atmosphere. These fields fluctuate from day to night, and from year to year, and they too are influenced by sunspots and in turn influence human health and life on earth.

Chapter Two

How Weather Sensitive Are You?

The house is still as his children tiptoe past Jeff's room. He is stretched out on the bed. The shades are drawn, but he still can't sleep. He's been tossing and turning most of the miserably wakeful night.

Outside the weather is lovely—a balmy, summer morning—but just five hours ago it was cold and miserable. Now, in spite of the fine weather, Jeff is unable to grab even a catnap. He's usually a good sleeper, but he does have nights like these and there seems no reason for it.

Down the street, Ira, a lawyer, has called in sick. After another night of stomach cramps and nausea, he tells his wife, "I don't understand it. I didn't eat anything unusual last night, but I feel as if I'm going to be sick any moment."

Jeff and Ira are worse off than Alma. She's the secretary at a life insurance office downtown and this day turns out to be a lulu. "I've made more mistakes in one hour than I did all last week," she tells her coworker, ripping a sheet out of the type-writer. "I feel confused and I keep forgetting things."

The Bensons, who work in the same office as Alma, came in in a tizzy. She's in a foul mood, and he's terribly anxious—but he's not sure what he is anxious about. "I just think I've forgotten something on that office building policy."

"You don't think," she snaps. "That's your trouble."

It's all over town. Grandma had a series of hot flashes. Billy doesn't want to go to school. Ellen can't eat, and the counter-man at the Blue Moon Diner is too dizzy to stand up. The service station attendant wonders whether he has had a heart attack. There's been something wrong with his breathing all morning.

What's going on? So many people are upset in one way or another, and yet there seems no obvious reason for it. This is a pleasant and prosperous place in middle America. Why, on a sunny, bright day, should so many people who live in it be miserable?

The clue to it all happened at four o'clock that morning. The weather had been unseasonably cold and unpleasant for a week. Then, abruptly, a warm air mass moved in and displaced the cold air. In less than an hour the temperature rose from 50° to 70° and the air pressure went up with it.

The clouds along the front passed as the sun rose. By mid-morning the town was bathed in sunshine, the dew was on the rose, all seemed right with the world—except for those unhappy people who were weather sensitive.

One of the troubling things about weather sensitivity is that it's not only a static weather condition that can trigger it, but a change in the weather as well. That the change is from good weather to bad or bad to good is irrelevant; it's the change itself that churns everybody up and lays them low. It was the change from bad to good weather that upset the people I described at the beginning of the chapter.

Weather sensitivity is a new phrase for a very old feeling.

All animals are weather sensitive. Squirrels grow fatter, birds migrate, and bears hibernate when the weather changes. Only mankind lacks a true understanding of weather language.

Clothes and houses, umbrellas and boots, air conditioning and central heating all give us a false sense of security. Humans believe that though the weather outside is frightful, inside it's most delightful—as if the weather outside had no influence. But no matter how secure you are inside, the weather outside has a very definite effect, especially if you are weather sensitive.

Most of us are interested in the weather. We glance at the morning headlines, and then our eyes drift up to the weather box in the corner of the newspaper. We switch on the radio in the morning to get the weather report along with the traffic flow, and at night we watch the weatherman or weatherwoman use satellite photos to tell us what to expect tomorrow.

We seem to be concerned with what to wear if it's cold, where to go if it snows. Will the roof leak if it rains? Should we take a chance and let the kids use the car if a fog moves in?

Americans do care about the weather, but the connection between how we feel, our physical and emotional health, and the weather, has rarely been considered seriously. Yet unconsciously most of us do make some connection. We meet a friend on the street. Usually we greet him with, "How are you?" We follow up with, "Isn't this a hell of a day?" And he answers, "Yeah, I hear they forecast a week of rain."

"Don't tell me! I feel depressed enough as it is."

Most of us know that on a wet, miserable day we feel miserable; on a bright, sunny day we feel good. These are just feelings, states of mind. Few of us are aware of how deeply the weather can affect physical and mental health.

In many respects Europe is far ahead of us in understanding that most people, to some degree, are weather sensitive, and—most important of all—that much can be done about it.

Weather can be a factor in heart disease, arthritis, allergies, eye problems, asthma, infections, and even cancer. It affects our mental health too. If a doctor can be warned in advance that with a certain type of weather his patients will be troubled, then he can take steps to help them. He can prescribe the proper medication, tell them what activities are good for them and what are bad. He can teach them to *listen to their own weather language.*

The Freiburg Experiment

A West German service, under the auspices of the government, has been set up in Freiburg-im-Breisgau linking medical practice and weather forecasting. I went there to find out how this system works.

Freiburg lies in the Rhine Valley, just where Germany's Black Forest begins. It is a modern, bustling university city, with a medieval overlay. Its importance to me was its status as the center of German experimentation in biometeorology. Here a research group instituted a system for monitoring the weather, interpreting its effects on human health, and, most uniquely, informing doctors and hospitals of those effects so they can offer patients better medical care.

I arrived at the Deutscher Wetterdienst (German Weather Service), took the elevator up nine floors, then walked an extra flight to Dr. Otmar Harflinger's office, tucked away beyond the elevator's reach. A slight, eager man in his late thirties, Dr. Harflinger is director of the Wetterdienst. He welcomed me enthusiastically.

"The project," he explained, "has worked out very well in certain areas. Where it has fallen down is financially." Physicians, he explained, are the same the world over, reluctant to pay for extra services and perhaps skeptical that this new science, biometeorology, is of much value.

"Do you honestly believe it is?" I asked.

"Oh, yes, I know it is. You must understand that one out of every three normal people—people who aren't sick, healthy people like you and me—are extremely weather sensitive. That's a tremendous number of people."

"And you can help them?"

"Of course. We can tell them when to take it easy, how to plan trips and vacations, and even what days to go out or stay indoors."

"But your service is for doctors only?"

Dr. Harflinger shrugged. "Perhaps someday it will be available to everyone. If our project here continues, if the government gives us funds, or if you in the United States take it up . . . There are many possibilities."

"You say that one person out of every three is weather sensitive. How did you find that out?"

"We advertised."

He laughed at my bewilderment. Perhaps I misunderstood him? No. His group, in order to locate research subjects, persuaded newspapers throughout Germany to print forms that people could fill out and send in to the Wetterdienst.

The form identifies weather sensitives. It covers one month. Twelve problems are listed. Each day the volunteer checks off which of them, if any, troubles him or her. When the forms are collected and matched against weather conditions for the month, a pattern emerges of who is weather sensitive, and to what degree.

"And the problems?" I asked.

He ticked them off on his finger. "One: general, allover tiredness. Two: heightened sensitivity to pain. Three: depression. Four: migraine. Five: headache. Six: disturbances in sleep. Seven: nervousness. Eight: pain in the joints. Nine: respiratory illness. Ten: asthmatic attacks. Eleven: back pain. Twelve: humidity."

"Humidity?"

"Well, an uncomfortable feeling when the air is humid."

(Later, talking to other researchers in Freiburg, I was able to add a number of other complaints of weather-sensitive people. They find it hard to concentrate. They forget things, feel confused, fatigued, ill humored, and generally sick. They may have hot flashes, and lose their appetite, have trouble with their vision, feel dizzy and breathless, and get pains in old scars and healed bones.)

"How does your system work?" I asked Dr. Harflinger. "How do you alert doctors, and what do you alert them to?"

Frowning a bit, he said, "Until last year we gave out little 'texts' when any doctor would call in, that is, any doctor who subscribed to our service. He would identify himself, and we would first tell him what the weather would be, the temperature, the humidity, the air pressure, what fronts are moving in or out, and, most important, if we expect any radical changes. Then we would tell him how much this particular kind of weather could affect weather-sensitive people. We first gave him the subjective impact of the weather on his patients and, finally, the physical impact."

"It sounds very thorough. Don't you do that anymore?"

"No," he sighed. "Now we just give them a warning, and we do that in code. Each doctor who subscribes to our service has a code of over forty physical problems. We tell him which of those problems are affected by the weather forecast. It's easier for us, but not as complete for the doctor."

"Why did you change your system?" I asked. "Weren't the medical 'texts' good enough?"

Dr. Harflinger shrugged. "They were much better than the code, but there were financial difficulties—government money and government bureaucracy."

"How useful do the medical people find your service?"

"Oh, we have some very enthusiastic subscribers."

"Did you ever think of offering this service to everyone instead of only doctors?" I asked.

As I asked the question, I imagined a television studio with a setting that was half weather studio and half doctor's office. In my fantasy, a weatherperson, dressed in a white coat to lend authority, would give the weather report, complete with all those weather maps that so few of us understand. Then he or she would turn to a set of anatomical charts. "Today the high-pressure zone over the Eastern states is bad for cardiac patients but good for asthmatics. All mental patients should be watched carefully. If you tend to be depressed, look for some fun people to spend the day with . . ."

My fantasy was shattered by Dr. Harflinger's answer.

"The general public tends to be oversubjective. Suggest a possible symptom, and they'll react to the suggestion. In other words, if you tell them today is bad for heart patients, they'll feel heart pains and flood the doctors' offices with alarmed calls."

I nodded, but I couldn't really believe him. I had heard the same excuse when I asked doctors why they didn't level with their patients and tell them exactly what was wrong. I don't believe that we lay people are too fragile to deal with the truth about health. I believe some doctors keep the truth from us to enhance their own prestige, to make themselves a bit more indispensable.

"We have done quite a bit of weather-connected research here," Dr. Harflinger told me, leafing through his papers. With funds supplied by Schering, the drug company, his group studied the effect of the weather on contrast media. Contrast media are used in X-ray examinations. Dr. Harflinger's group found that when weather conditions are extreme, some patients are badly affected by contrast media. Knowing this, there are certain days they should not be examined by X ray.

In another study, Dr. Harflinger and his associates have set up a controlled climate chamber where they can duplicate virtually any weather condition—hot, cold, humid, dry, high in pressure or low. Here they give psychological tests to people under different weather conditions. The tests are still in progress, but eventually they hope to learn just what kind of weather makes us bright and perceptive and what kind makes us dull or uncomprehending.

Dr. Harflinger also told me of a study in progress at the Mercedes-Benz auto plant in Stuttgart, linking accidents with the weather.

I became intrigued as I looked over Dr. Harflinger's other data and jotted down names of people to talk to and avenues to explore.

As I got ready to leave, I stood up and winced as I straightened. "A bad back," I explained.

Dr. Harflinger nodded sympathetically. "The weather?"

I looked out the window at the bright summer day and said, "I don't think so. It's too nice out."

"Ah, that's the problem. You're probably weather sensitive, and you must realize that it's not the weather at the moment that matters, but the weather change that just took place. Yesterday and for three days before that it was cold and wet. Last night a warm air mass moved in. Change. Any abrupt change after a static period causes weather-sensitive people to react."

"I find that hard to believe."

He laughed. "Oh, yes, it's hard to believe, but it's true. A change to bad weather or a change to good—the change is what causes the problem."

I left, hoping for a week of nice weather with no change.

How to Discover Your Own Weather Sensitivity

Are you extremely weather sensitive, moderately weather sensitive, or only slightly sensitive? Here is a chart that will help you to discover your own sensitivity.

Use the chart to keep a record of your symptoms for an entire month. The numbers on the left side of the chart indicate the days of the month. Across the top is a list of typical symptoms of weather sensitivity. The last column on the right is for you to mark weather changes.

If you feel any of the symptoms listed, put an X in the box

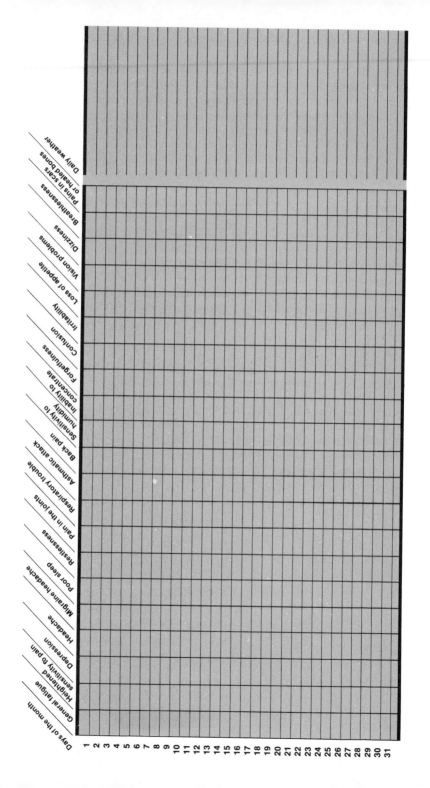

Days of the month	General fatigue	Heightened sensitivity to pain	Depression	Headache	Migraine headache	Poor sleep	Restlessness	Pain in the joints	Respiratory trouble	Asthmatic attack	Back pain	Sensitivity to humidity	Inability to concentrate	Forgetfulness	Confusion	Irritability	Loss of appetite	Vision problems	Dizziness	Breathlessness	Pains in scars or healed bones	Daily weather
1																						
2																						
3																						
4																						
5																						
6																						
7																						
8																						
9																						
10																						
11																						
12																						
13																						
14																						
15																						
16																						
17																						
18																						
19																						
20																						
21																						
22																						
23																						
24																						
25																						
26																						
27																						
28																						
29																						
30																						
31																						

SOME FREQUENTLY USED WEATHER-CHART MARKINGS TO HELP YOU FILL IN YOUR WEATHER CHART

▼▼▼▼▼	Cold Front
⌒⌒⌒	Warm Front
▼⌒▼⌒	Stationary Front
⌒▼⌒▼⌒▼	Occluded Front
○	Clear
Ⓡ	Rain
◑	Partly Cloudy
●	Cloudy
Ⓣ	Thunderstorms
Ⓢ	Snow

Ⓕ	Fog
Ⓩ	Freezing Rain
∿	Hurricane

Wind Force *(only significant forces noted)*

○—	Strong Wind
○—	Moderate Gale
○—	Gale

Direction of Wind

○↓	East Wind
○↑	West Wind

Note: Many newspapers use their own set of symbols, different from the standard ones shown above. Fortunately, there is usually a key given on the map itself.

under that symptom across from the day on which it's felt.

In the weather column, note with an X any significant weather change.

The change that seems to cause the greatest trouble to weather-sensitive people is the passage of fronts with their associated atmospheric turbulence. Some people are affected by cold fronts—others by warm, stationary, or occluded fronts.

Check your weather report, the map in your daily paper, or the radio or television announcements for the important front changes. If a change occurs, mark an X on that day.

The second most important weather problem in terms of sensitivity is the combination of heat and humidity. For weather-sensitive people, any day with a temperature-humidity index (THI) of 73 or over should be marked on the chart.

If the THI is not included in your weather report, the following temperatures and humidities will tell you what days to mark.

If the temperature is:	And the humidity is over:
75°	65 percent
80°	45 percent
85°	30 percent
90°	10 percent

Above 90°, mark that day no matter what the humidity!

Any day with a significantly falling barometer should be marked.

Mark any day with a wind strong enough to bend large branches on trees, make telephone wires whistle, and give you trouble with an umbrella. If you know the wind velocity, mark any day with a wind over 30 miles per hour—*particularly dry, hot winds!*

Mark any day with a severe thunderstorm with electrical displays.

If sunspots are reported, mark the following day.

At the end of the month, match your X's against the weather conditions.

If you experienced any *one* symptom consistently during a weather change, you are at least somewhat weather sensitive. The number of your symptoms will show your degree of sensitivity. *Three* symptoms that match weather changes means you are markedly weather sensitive. *More than three* means you are extremely weather sensitive.

A New Type of Weather Service

Charting your own weather sensitivity is an important step in learning weather language. Equally important is making the connection between sensitivity and the weather.

I believe that in America, with all the facilities at our command, we should have a service similar to that in Freiburg. I don't believe that such a service should be available only to physicians. The German doctors to whom I talked were enthusiastic about the reports, though some felt they did not have time to alert patients to the dangers of risky weather patterns.

Doctors in the United States are just as busy; it would be foolish to expect them to call each of their patients with a warning every time there was a significant weather change.

But a weather and health service, like Freiburg's, designed for the general public, would be very valuable. We are already warned when pollution levels are unsafe, even though these warnings are of most value to people with heart and respiratory disease. We know, however, that pollution can be a hazard to us all; we would like to know at what level, and in what way.

The average healthy, if weather-sensitive, person reacts to pollution. He may react seriously or lightly. He may have trouble with his eyes; they can become red and irritated. He may have a nagging headache. Breathing may become

SOME TYPICAL CHARTS FILLED IN FOR A ONE-MONTH PERIOD.
Weather-Sensitivity Chart for Naomi T.

Her occasional loss of appetite does not relate to weather changes, but Naomi is weather sensitive. She has pain in her joints the day before certain weather changes, and during them. Even with only one symptom being weather-related, her consistency is significant.

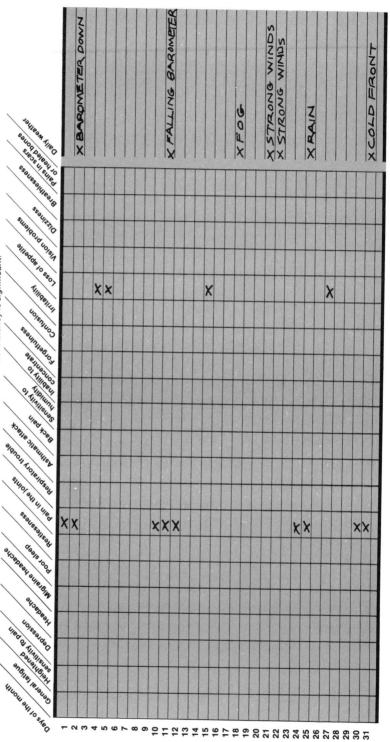

SOME TYPICAL CHARTS FILLED IN FOR A ONE-MONTH PERIOD.
Weather-Sensitivity Chart for Anne W.

Anne is extremely weather sensitive. There is a very close correlation between her symptoms and weather changes.

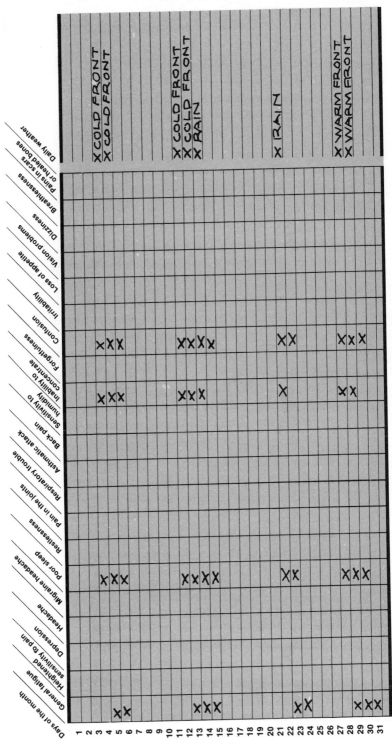

SOME TYPICAL CHARTS FILLED IN FOR A ONE-MONTH PERIOD.
Weather-Sensitivity Chart for Barney R.

Barney is not a weather sensitive. The correlation between symptoms and weather changes is weak and inconsistent.

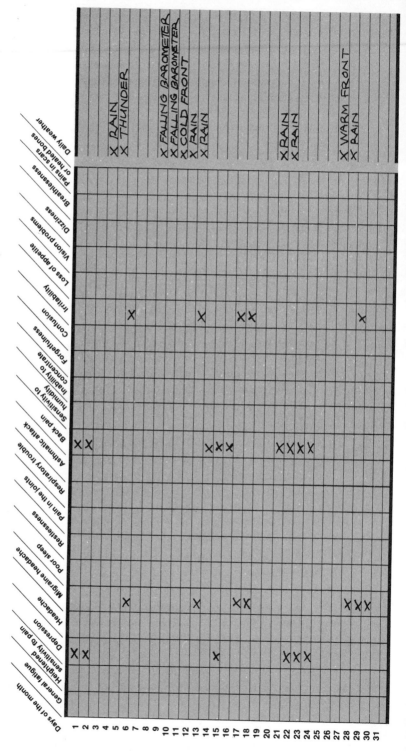

difficult. The nose can become inflamed and sore. The weather report that tells you that the air is polluted should also warn you of these possible reactions—if only to set your mind at ease that you are not coming down with some more serious illness.

This new service should not be a telephone call-in operation as in Germany, charging subscribers for each use. Instead it should be a part of the regular television, radio, or newspaper coverage of the weather. The basic information could be fed to each station by the federal Department of Health, Education, and Welfare. Each station should have a consulting or resident biometeorologist to interpret the daily weather patterns locally and decide what effect each has on heart disease, respiratory disease, cancer, asthma, psychiatric problems, and all the other pathological conditions known to be affected by the weather.

The service could also determine just how much the weather would affect weather-sensitive persons. Along with the daily weather report, we would then get a rundown on what we should avoid—if we are weather sensitive—and what we can safely do.

Such a service would be of great importance for the medical profession. It would make doctors and hospitals aware of the weather-health connection and of the surge in weather-related diseases when the weather changes.

It's not difficult to imagine how such a weather service would work. My little fantasy, as I listened to Dr. Harflinger in Freiburg, could easily be expanded. Let's call the service WEATHER, an acronym for Weather Effects And The HEalth Reaction. Since television is the most popular medium, we can start there.

The local weatherperson says, after some appropriate fiddling with charts and satellite photos, "It will remain warm and muggy across the Eastern seaboard today, tonight, and tomorrow. Temperatures will range from the high eighties inland to the seventies at the shore, but it will feel much warmer because of the high humidity. Showers or thunderstorms can be expected."

Then he adds, "But before you get out your galoshes and umbrellas, let's hear from Dr. Jones, our resident biometeorologist."

The camera pulls back to include Dr. Jones, who now proceeds to interpret the weather's effect on health. "For all of us, the high temperatures combined with humidity are a potential danger. Try to avoid any work that will keep you out in the sun—or for that matter any physically strenuous work. Your stamina will be much lower because of the high humidity.

"If you have to do physical work, take frequent breaks. Make sure you get enough water and spike your food with some extra salt.

"This is a bad day for all cardiac patients. Stay indoors, if you can, and keep the air conditioner going.

"If you have arthritis or any form of rheumatism, remember to stay dry. Take your umbrella and rainshoes if you go out.

"Hay-fever sufferers may enjoy a respite for the next day or so. Rainstorms often clear the air of pollen and pollution—but watch those electrical discharges. There may be an excess of positive ions in the air. Headache sufferers—keep the aspirin handy."

Another typical forecast might come from the Midwest. "A strong cold front is moving eastward. We can expect showers and thunderstorms, and then sunny, cool weather."

The biometeorologist would add, "This is a particularly trying time for all weather-sensitive people. The front with its attendant turbulence can bring out vague aches and pains, headaches, anxiety, and irritability. This is a good time to be wary of getting involved in complicated business deals. People are a bit more apt to look for trouble, and therefore to find it, during the passage of fronts.

"For rheumatic patients, this is a bad time. The various

pressure changes brought on by the passing front can cause arthritic flare-ups. Cut down on activity and stay warm."

Or a typical winter forecast from the inland Northwest: "The thermometer sank to a new low this morning with temperatures ranging from zero to ten above in the city and minus five or lower in the surrounding countryside. The air is cold and crisp, the sky clear, and the THI at a comfortable fifty percent. There is a static high over the area that should remain for at least four or five days."

The biometeorologist adds, "Most weather-sensitive listeners can lean back with a sigh of relief. The absence of any weather change for the next few days should give you a comfortable period. This is a time to get things done if you bundle up against the cold.

"Cardiac patients, beware! The extra stress of the cold can be damaging to the heart. Don't overexert yourself. If you must go out, be sure to guard your chest and mouth. Breathing cold air may be dangerous.

"Allergy sufferers should have a respite now—unless you're allergic to the cold. Watch for any unexplained rashes on exposed areas."

These are brief samples of weather reports with biometeorological effects. There are so many weather patterns that affect us in so many different ways that it would be impossible to list all. The few I've given are typical and indicate how such a service could help not only the seriously ill, but the average healthy weather-sensitive person as well.

I want to emphasize that although weather is a very important factor in disease, it is not the only factor. Weather does not cause disease, but it does influence it. Weather does not produce weather-sensitive people. Their sensitivity is a function of their own makeup, but weather does influence them. It does make them feel any number of troubling complaints.

Fortunately, until we have a weather service like the one

I've described, we can make do with the existing daily reports. This book will detail the known impact of the weather on healthy weather-sensitive people and on people with various illnesses. It will suggest what you can do about these effects.

How? Just check today's weather report. List all significant weather changes. Are there major barometric fluctuations expected? If there is an area of low barometric pressure, it is significant. If a front is due to pass over, or has just passed over, that's significant. Heat and humidity are important, as are extreme cold, winds (especially hot, dry ones), and thunderstorms.

If you have filled out the earlier weather-sensitivity chart, you know how sensitive you are. You can turn to the chapters in the book that explain the effects of each weather change on weather sensitives and you'll know what to expect. You can then anticipate any impact on your life: whether it's going to be a good day or a bad day for making serious decisions or taking actions with far-reaching implications.

Put off whatever you can if it's a bad day; if you can't put things off, approach them carefully. Question your own judgment.

If you suffer from any disease, note with particular care the chapter in the book about the weather's impact on that disease. You'll learn what to avoid, what to do, and what to watch for.

Some doctors, when I discussed this with them, felt very enthusiastic about such a service; others wondered if it would produce many imaginary ailments. What it would do, I am sure, is increase our knowledge of our own weather sensitivity. I'm convinced that the ability to interpret weather language in terms of our own health and emotions will yield far more benefits than possible disadvantages.

Weather influences all of us—how we feel and how we relate to other people. Weather is only one of many factors in the human condition, but a very important one. Weather sensitivity is a highly individual condition. In the long run only the individual, through observation and knowledge, can understand his or her own reaction—and interpret that very personal weather language.

How Weather Affects the Inner Body

In Leiden, the Netherlands, Dr. S. W. Tromp, a geophysicist and physiologist, heads the Biometeorological Research Center. Dr. Tromp, a dedicated and enthusiastic scientist, has collected a staggering amount of data concerning the weather's impact on man. His research is overwhelming in its detailed concern with every possible element of weather and health.

As I became more and more involved with the effect of weather on the human body, I was constantly faced with questions. What is the mechanism of its action? Why do certain winds cause irritability and sleeplessness? Why do more people die when a front passes? Why are babies born in March more liable to have birth defects? Why do these things and so many others occur—and how?

In Dr. Tromp's research I found hints of the complex physiological process behind all these inexplicable occurrences. As I became more familiar with his work I saw that there was an obvious answer. The weather and all its elements affect certain basic and important regulatory systems in our bodies. Heat, cold, humidity, air pressure, ultraviolet light, pollutants, ozone, ions, sferics—these and other weather phenomena had an impact on the hypothalamus, the rhinencephalon, the pituitary, the parasympathetic nervous system, the thyroid, the serotonin release mechanism, and other parts of the body.

In order to understand how this happens we have to know a little about the workings of these organs and processes. The *hypothalamus* is that portion of the brain that controls, among other things, the digestion, the amount of water retained in the body, body temperature, and how we sleep.

The front of the hypothalamus tells us when to lose heat by sweating or opening our capillaries, while the back of it keeps us from getting cold by making us shiver or by narrowing our capillaries.

Our capillaries—those little blood vessels next to the skin—can cool the blood when they're open wide or conserve body heat when they contract. If they narrow on a cold day, they protect us against losing body heat; on a hot day their narrowing keeps us from absorbing heat.

The hypothalamus also affects the *parasympathetic nervous system*, a part of the involuntary nervous system. It furnishes signals to those organs like the heart, the eyes, the lungs, and the stomach that work automatically, not when we will them to.

The *pituitary* gland is a small, oval structure attached to the base of the skull, a gland vitally important to all aspects of growth, maturation, and reproduction. It regulates the body's hormones, including those that control metabolism, water retention, and sexual functioning.

The *rhinencephalon* is the area of the brain that controls the sense of smell. It is linked to the hypothalamus.

The *thyroid* gland in the throat regulates overall body metabolism.

Serotonin is a chemical found in the blood and other parts of the body. Too much of it causes our blood vessels to constrict and changes the way the nervous system works. In excess it can cause migraine headaches, heart palpitations, stress, and many other symptoms.

Almost every weather element works on one or more of these systems or glands to one degree or another. As an example, Dr. Tromp suggests that we consider ultraviolet light. Too much of it produces severe sunburn, and the toxins thereby released into the body can cause the pituitary gland to release hormones that in turn affect the digestive tract, cause blood pressure to drop, and increase red cells, hemoglobin, calcium, and phosphates.

Too little ultraviolet light adversely affects the thyroid gland and can send shock waves through every part of the body.

Other examples are easy to find. The stress of heat and cold can affect the hypothalamus and the pituitary gland, and whatever affects these two affects our entire system.

Pollens and man-made pollutants, carried by the winds or held stationary by temperature inversions, can stimulate the rhinencephalon and affect the emotions and moods, the heart, the digestive system, and the glands.

Winds can carry ozone down to earth, and ozone can stimulate the rhinencephalon and in turn the hypothalamus. Again, its effects can shake up the entire body.

Positive and negative ions (and these can be produced by winds, electrical storms, and even cigarette smoke) can cause the release of serotonin, an excess of which upsets the entire body.

In addition to ions, there is a constant electrical field in our atmosphere. Rain, snow, fog, and thunder are some of the weather elements that can cause this field to fluctuate. Strong sferics released from the electrical field seem able to throw the parasympathetic nervous system out of whack and influence the brain as well. (The brain, remember, contains the hypothalamus and the rhinencephalon.) Most important of all, there is a constant feedback and interconnection between all of these organs. Considering all this, it seems logical that even the slightest fluctuation in weather should affect the sensitive among us. The wonder is that we can survive so many weather changes so well.

At any rate, these are the main pathways of weather sensitivity that Dr. Tromp and his associates have uncovered. There are undoubtedly many more, but surely these are enough to explain how a hot, dry wind or a cold, bitter day or a passing front do what they do to some of us.

Fortunately there are things we can do to mitigate the effects of the weather on us, and we'll come to that in the course of the book.

Chapter Three

How Weather Changes Affect You

Looking across an open valley at a line of far-off mountains, we can see everything clearly—every tree, every field, every house for miles and miles. We can even see the cars winding along the dusty roads. It is hard to believe that the valley is not empty, that in the air above it, even while we watch, there may be an unseen battle, a meteorological skirmish between two air masses.

Such battles go on constantly in the great weather war around the globe. A cold air mass moves in and challenges a warm one. Along an immense front there are vast atmospheric upheavals, ups and downs of hot and cold air, until eventually the cold air mass drives the warm one out, and the atmosphere settles down to a period of cold weather and high pressure. If the warm air mass wins, the weather stays warm, and the barometer may fall.

In any war, victory is often determined by the force in reserve that an army can draw up. In the atmospheric war, victory depends on the force behind the air mass, or on which air mass is moving and which is stationary; victory usually goes to the moving one.

We are always concerned with the outcome of the struggle between air masses, even though we may be unaware of the struggle itself. The outcome determines what weather we will have—hot or cold, dry or wet, high pressure or low pressure. But in truth we should be concerned with the struggle because its result determines what we're going to feel. The meteorological war is really an ever-changing movement and mixture of masses of air. Those of us who are weather sensitive feel that change. We feel it with headaches or anxiety or any one, or more, of the other forty-odd symptoms that go to make us that way.

The war in the air can go on for an entire day and night before there is a winner, and the invading armies of hot or cold air push the defeated masses out. Among the casualties of the war are all those tormented weather sensitives who experienced the change in their bodies. Weather sensitives react to any change, and they react during and immediately after the change. If the weather has been stable for three or four days before the change, their reaction is even stronger. If the change is a violent and sudden one—you know, those hot days that suddenly turn cold, or those cold, bitter days that warm up in a few hours—then their reaction is just as sudden, just as violent.

How Fronts Affect You

No matter how strong a front is, its ability to affect a weather sensitive depends, in part, on the sensitive's reaction. Tom may be able to sail through a mild front with no discomfort, but let the front be a strong one and he has spells of dizziness and spots dance in front of his eyes. His neighbor Dick, on the other hand, has an erratic heartbeat at the first sign of a mild front, but a very strong front doesn't bother him. Harry, down the block, is weather sensitive, too. The poor fellow reacts to every change—strong, moderate, or weak. Let the weather only hint at change and Harry is exhausted, thoroughly and completely.

It is not only the fact of change that affects such sensitives; it's the speed of the change, the amount of change, and the barometric rise or fall once a front passes. Barometric movements are usually signaled by a shift in the velocity and direction of the winds. Other signs are the amount and duration of rain, and electric disturbances in the air.

We now know both the changes that disturb weather sensitives and their reactions. The Freiburg researchers have found over forty symptoms they display, and other scientists have studied the blood chemistry and circulatory and respiratory systems of healthy weather sensitives and come up with some unusual facts.

Blood cells change with the barometric pressure. The white cells increase in number when the barometer falls sharply, and blood clots more quickly just before a cold front passes, while the clots formed are stronger afterwards. The amount of blood in the body decreases and the blood sedimentation rate is lower after the passage of a cold front.

As for the circulatory system, we face a greater risk of forming embolisms (sudden and potentially fatal obstructions of blood vessels) on days when either cold or warm fronts pass over, and the blood flows through the capillaries more easily after cold fronts, less easily after warm fronts.

This is logical: We need a freer blood flow in cold weather to warm us up. In animal studies the metabolism of the muscles is found to be high after cold fronts, low after warm fronts, and that too is understandable. We need to burn more energy in cold weather since we lose heat more readily. But it is harder to figure out why we should urinate more often once a cold front passes, or why digitalis should work on the heart better when the barometer falls sharply, why morphine's effect is much stronger at that time, and why we secrete more nitrogen and phosphoric acid when cold fronts go over.

We do not understand these reactions; at this point one can only see them as further illustrations of the effects that weather has on healthy men and women. The changes listed here— only a fraction of the physical changes that take place when the weather changes—happen to all of us, sick and healthy, weather-insensitive people as well as weather-sensitive people.

Dos and Don'ts

Weather-sensitive people are not all the same. Some react only to fronts, some only to heat, and others only to winds. Each weather-sensitive person may be selective in his or her reaction—but it is also possible for a weather-sensitive person to react to every weather change, or to three, or four, or five or any number.

If you react to fronts, is there anything you can do to lessen the effect? Unfortunately, not much. You can block out rain and get out of the wind. You can bundle up against the cold and cool off with air conditioners when it's too hot. But there seems no defense, outside of pressurized rooms, against atmospheric highs and lows.

The typical weather sensitive who lives in a turbulent area should keep on top of predicted weather changes. Watch the TV weatherperson and listen closely when he or she explains the weather map. On the day after the front moves in, try not to make important decisions at home and in the office.

If you're fortunate enough to be only mildly weather sensitive, be aware of the people around you who are more directly affected. If your boss complains of headaches and they seem to come after a front passes, don't pick that day to discuss the new advertising campaign or to ask for a raise. If your wife or husband has unaccountable attacks of irritability, and you can tie them to the passage of fronts, don't pick that day to criticize or analyze.

Some physicians have treated weather-sensitive people with analgesics to cut down on the pain; others have used stimulants to keep them going in spite of the pain. The best that can be done is to treat the symptoms of weather-sensitive people. Give them medication for their particular symptoms—aspirin for headache, cafergot for migraine, mild sedatives for sleeplessness, and so on.

Beyond this, the weather-sensitive person who is miserable might try to move to a location with a minimum of frontal activity. Coastal areas and islands experience less daily and seasonal temperature variation than inland areas and are warmer in winter and cooler in summer. But there is more air turbulence at the coast; fronts, as they go inland, lose their punch, so inland areas are calmer. Mountain climates, too, are usually calmer and freer of air turbulence.

If you are weather sensitive and you cannot move, if you frown on tranquilizers and pep pills, if nothing seems to work, then you are in trouble, for the one thing about the weather that is certain is that it always changes, and that's what an exquisitely weather-sensitive person needs least.

The Cruel Winds

Some four hundred years ago the great Swiss physician and alchemist Paracelsus stated, "He who knows the origin of the winds, of thunder, and of the weather also knows where diseases come from." He could have added, "And why weather-sensitive people shudder when the winds blow," for they do. Like the movement of fronts, some winds can put weather-sensitive people through every agony known to biometeorology. In fact, these same winds can also affect people who usually are not weather sensitive.

Winds blow hot and cold, and it's a toss-up which is worse.

Statistics show that when cold polar winds sweep down on the land, there is an increase in the number of heart attacks. Anginal pain gets worse and blood pressure shoots up because the heart must work harder to keep the body warm.

Psychological tests given while hot winds were blowing have turned up some good news and some bad news about the relations among winds, personality, and ability. The bad news first: Hot winds make people more neurotic and irritable, and then they do worse in intelligence tests. They can't understand mechanical instructions as well as they can in cooler weather.

The good news: Hot winds won't keep you from doing your best in math and clerical work, nor will it affect your visual perception.

Some winds are lovely, cool, and refreshing—poets' winds, warm west winds. But others are terrible—veritable monsters. Europe's foehn is one of these. In medieval times, people thought the foehn blew in from Phoenicia, and they named it the "Phoenicias," then shortened that to foehn. This hot, dry terror is not only deadly in a biometeorological sense, but in a physical sense as well. It blows in from Italy loaded with wet, humid air, drops its moisture on the Swiss Alps, and then, warm and dry, sweeps down into the northern reaches of the land. As it blows, it warms the mountain snow and causes avalanches.

Albert is a resident of Bad Tölz, a town in Germany in the foothills of the Alps. I talked to him about the foehn, and he shook his head sadly. "Some reporters from Munich came here a few years ago to talk about the foehn, and they told us it was all in our heads. But they didn't understand. They weren't here while it was blowing. Everyone in the village was upset. You couldn't talk to your neighbor, or if you did, you snapped at him. We were all on edge.

"Every night while the foehn was blowing, I'd have trouble sleeping—the nightmares. And I'd wake up with a headache. My sister—she hemorrhaged the day before it started.

"It seems to go on forever, day after day. It's so dry. You

sweat, and the sweat is just pulled out of you by the wind. We were all thirsty. My God, the beer we consumed!"

"How does it start?" I asked.

"It starts with warm air over the cold ground. At first it's wet before the real blowing begins, and once it comes it goes on for weeks. In our street there was one suicide, and I put it down to that devil wind. And it's not only sickness and upset. My cousin who works in a factory in Munich told me there were more accidents during the weeks of the foehn than for months and months before or after."

Albert's report had the ring of truth, and I had additional scientific confirmation of the foehn's deadly quality from other sources. A psychiatrist told me that in mental institutions there were almost one-quarter more patients with problems when the foehn struck. An internist in another Alpine town told me that he had at least one-third more complaints during foehn days.

Why the foehn affects people is still not clear. Some researchers believe the hot, dry wind creates an enormous number of positive ions because of the friction of its descent down the Alps. Positive ions have been held to be the cause of many upsets, and Dr. W. Morikofer tried to test this with ion-testing apparatus. He reported, however, that he couldn't duplicate the foehn's action.

Other researchers feel that certain people have nervous systems particularly vulnerable to hot, dry winds—that, in fact, these are our weather-sensitive people.

Other European winds are hard on the people in their paths. The warm, dry autan blows up the Rhone Valley in France and it is accompanied by low-pressure systems. Babies are usually the first to react: They run high temperatures and suffer dehydration, become restless, and can't sleep. Some children don't do well in school when the autan blows, and others suffer respiratory troubles, colds, and asthma.

Weather-sensitive adults react strongly to the autan, almost as strongly as they do to the foehn. Quarrels, insomnia, heart attacks, and migraines are typical autan symptoms.

The mistral is another Rhone Valley wind, but unlike the autan it is cold and dry. This strong wind, however, is still ugly in its effects. Like the foehn, the mistral causes migraine and insomnia and is dreaded by weather sensitives.

There are other "killer" winds around the world; in Africa and Asia the simooms are hot, dry desert winds. In India there is the bhoot. In the Mediterranean countries there is the sirocco, in Spain the solano. And so it blows all through Europe, Asia, and even Australia, where they have the brick-fielder. This wind earned its colorful name by blowing clouds of dust from the brickfields. After a while it was renamed the southerly buster.

Israel has its own killer wind, the sharav. It is heated up by the desert sands, and it brings with it depression, headache, irritation, and respiratory upset.

Here in America we have few natural deadly winds, perhaps because of the geography of our country. Winds on the Pacific Northwest Coast blow wet against the Rockies, then dry and sometimes hot down the landward side. The chinook is one such, and it causes almost as many problems as its European cousin, the foehn. In southern California, the Santa Ana wind has a deadly reputation. When it blows across Los Angeles its heat and dryness seem to cause an enormous increase in crime.

Many winds are given names to personify them, and perhaps as an ancient way of pacifying them. You can plead with a named object, wind, or mountain or storm god, and you can ask it to spare you. The chinook was named after an Indian tribe, and in the United States we name our hurricanes. But the old practice of giving them women's names has been replaced, after protest, by naming them alternately for men and women.

Hurricanes are killer winds, but their destructive power lies in the physical damage they can do. They will lift houses, turn over cars, and destroy entire communities. We respect

them for this, but we may have winds that are just as dangerous and, for some, even more dangerous. Because they are
gentle winds or soft winds, we ignore them.

Dr. H. B. Schultz studied the disposal of agricultural wastes
in northern California and found that the "monsoonlike in-
flow of oceanic air" cleaned the air over the nearby cities.
However, in the fall, when 1.5 million tons of rice straw have
to be burned for pest control, these same winds can blow the
burning pollutants over the nearby cities. This cleansing
wind then becomes a deadly one.

In Colorado, there is a vast nuclear installation at Rocky
Flats. A gentle wind blows from Rocky Flats towards Denver,
and an area near the city in the path of the wind has recorded
twice as many cases of leukemia and lung cancer as one would
normally expect. Here another harmless wind has been turned
into a killer by our own efforts.

When nature fails to provide us with the winds like the foehn
and the mistral we seem to create our own.

Dos and Don'ts

If you are very weather sensitive, and you live in an area
where the winds are deadly, try to get away during the windy
season. If this is not possible, at least recognize the effect of
the winds. Listen to the weather language that your body
speaks. Link your symptoms to the wind.

If you are wind sensitive, be wary when the cruel winds
blow. If you are in a factory job, on a construction site, or any
place where there is a danger of physical accidents, take extra
care.

All drivers of cars and trucks should realize that these
winds can affect the judgment of even slightly weather-sensitive people. Drive with extra care at such times.

If your children are being tested in school, and you live in
or near one of these windy areas, try to keep them away from

any verbal intelligence tests, but let them go to school for math testing.

If your car breaks down during one of the killer wind periods, wait until the wind passes before taking it in to be fixed. There is a one-in-three chance that the garage mechanic may himself be affected by the weather, and his mechanical ability may be impaired.

Remember that everyone is affected by these winds to a greater or lesser extent. This is a time for charity in personal relationships.

If you cannot escape the wind, there are drugs that can help you over the worst time. Consult your doctor. He can help you sleep better, lower your irritation threshold, and banish your headaches. He can also monitor any heart or lung problems the weather causes. If he fails you, a few aspirins may well do wonders.

When cold winds blow and you must go out, dress warmly and wear a windproof hat and coat. A face mask of porous wool will keep you from inhaling air cold enough to damage your lungs.

Remember that when "killer" winds blow, it is a bad time for emotional involvement, for making legal decisions, important purchases, financial deals; in short, avoid any weighty judgments during the hot, dry, windy weather.

Even if you yourself are not weather sensitive, remember that your family, your friends and lovers, and your acquaintances and business associates might be troubled. Listen to their weather language and try to take their weather sensitivity into account.

How Altitudes Affect You

On a recent flight to Europe, I listened to the stewardess explain the workings of an oxygen mask to be used in case of an emergency. I didn't listen too carefully. I've flown before, and the cabin was comfortably pressurized. My ears didn't even pop as we rose. But the very comfort of the plane cabin set me thinking, and I remembered an experiment conducted during World War II.

In those days air force pilots often flew by instinct as much as by charts. Cabins weren't pressurized then, and if a plane went above a certain height, oxygen masks had to be used. Because of the awkwardness of the masks, the air force decided to try different techniques to teach their pilots to survive in thin air.

"People who live in high altitudes learn to compensate," one of the researchers said. "Why don't we teach our men how to breathe properly?"

"If they can do it," a major said doubtfully. "You know about the farmer who wanted to lift his cows? He started practicing by lifting a ten-pound weight and he added a half pound a day. He figured he'd adapt easily. He reached one hundred sixty pounds and collapsed."

There was a general laugh, but the researchers decided to proceed with the experiment. They trained a man to breathe differently, to take deep breaths at twice his normal rate. When he became accomplished at this, they sent him up in a plane with a group of men who had no breathing training.

As the plane rose higher and higher, the cabin air grew thinner. At 15,000 feet everyone put on his oxygen mask. At 24,000 feet all but the pilot were told to take them off. In a few minutes all lost consciousness except the man who had been trained to breathe rapidly. He remasked the unconscious men, and for over an hour he moved around the plane and carried on his normal duties with no oxygen mask.

On a later flight, a pilot trained in the same technique flew his plane at 24,000 feet for half an hour with no mask.

The remarkable thing about this experiment is that at 15,000 feet the air becomes too thin and cold for comfortable normal breathing. At 18,000 feet the discomfort becomes pain and at 24,000 feet a person without oxygen loses consciousness quickly. The trained breathers had no trouble.

"Breathing," the doubting air force major had to admit after the experiment, "is not like lifting weights."

And yet in a way it is. There is a limit at which our lungs and circulatory system can operate. No matter how fast we breathe, we cannot get enough oxygen if there isn't enough available. The only solution would be to have more lung capacity. The science-fiction writers who recognized this gave their Martian characters huge chests. If Mars had a breathable atmosphere, they reasoned, it would have to be very thin and the Martians would have to be very chesty.

And yet, in spite of this, we know that men can live comfortably at 24,000 feet, even men used to the pressure at sea level. Just think of all the mountaineers who have lived for weeks above 24,000 feet. The answer is that they climb to that height slowly. As they climb, as the air pressure decreases, as the air becomes thinner and the oxygen supply diminishes, their bodies unconsciously begin to train themselves much as the air force pilot was trained, and they breathe deeper and faster.

In breathing, we take in oxygen and get rid of carbon dioxide, but we must keep a certain amount of carbon dioxide in our bodies. It stimulates the breathing center; without it we would stop breathing. A problem arises here because deep, fast breathing washes the carbon dioxide out of our lungs.

A while back, there was a college craze called hyperventilation. Young people would breathe rapidly and deeply until they keeled over unconscious. The reason was simple. They washed the carbon dioxide out of their system with their rapid breathing.

Our mountaineering friends increase their breathing slowly and their bodies have a chance to adjust, but it's a difficult adjustment. The acid-alkaline balance of our body shifts because it is maintained in part by carbon dioxide. So even though we increase our oxygen intake, we decrease our carbon dioxide and walk a thin line. Breathe too little and you don't get enough oxygen; breathe too much and you don't have enough carbon dioxide.

The mountaineer goes up slowly, but sometimes visitors to the mountains go up much more quickly. Cars ascend at a rapid rate and trains in the Andes go from sea level to over 13,000 feet in less than a day. The traveler taking either of these routes usually gets sluggish and loses all energy. He may develop a headache and a racing heartbeat, grow pale and nauseated, and even vomit. All these are symptoms of *oxygen starvation.*

Eventually, the newcomer to the mountains, whether he arrived by train, car, or in easy stages by climbing, becomes acclimated. His sleep may be troubled for a while, and he may not be up to heavy exertion, but he does get along. If he goes higher up, above 21,000 feet, however, he may not get along too well. A long stay at that altitude and he'll lose weight, appetite and strength, be unable to think clearly, and suffer low blood pressure. The problem may be oxygen starvation or exhaustion of the adrenal glands. Whatever it is, it's not good.

Legend has it that most of the Spanish conquerers of Peru were infertile for generations in that upland climate. Some historians feel that their sperm couldn't develop properly without oxygen. Others, however, say the infertility was due to the syphilis and gonorrhea that ran rampant through their ranks. On the other hand the native Peruvians, who have lived in the mountains their whole lives, have had no trouble with infertility or illness. They can exert themselves without gasping. In sports, mountain people have an advantage over lowlanders as long as the games are played on their own turf. Their adaptation started before birth. They were born able to cope with thin air.

Babies born in mountain areas of lowland parents have a high incidence of ductus arteriosus, a birth defect in which a blood vessel that should close at birth, when the baby transfers from the liquid environment of the womb to the gaseous environment of air, fails to close. Such a defect causes the blood to recirculate through the lungs instead of the body. The body is starved for oxygen, blue and cyanotic.

The bodies of mountain people are different in subtle ways. Their lung capacity is often greater, their pulse and respiration faster, their body chemistry slightly different, and they have more red blood cells to carry more oxygen.

A study by Dr. A. R. Frisancho, in the journal *Human Biology,* on how humans adapt to high altitudes suggests that people born in the mountains don't depend on extra-fast breathing to make up the oxygen lack. Their lungs are simply larger and there is more of an area for oxygen to be taken from the air. It's an interesting exploration of the nature versus nurture theory. Do they develop large lungs because of the thin air, or are they born with large lungs and better able to survive? Do small-lunged babies simply not live? Dr. Frisancho says only, "The earlier the age, the greater the influence of the environment."

Someday babies born in the highlands of newly arrived parents will be compared to babies born of native highland parents and we may have answers to the question.

Another fact about high altitude comes from the investigations of Drs. N. A. Little and J. N. Hanna reported in the *International Journal of Biometeorology.* They studied cold stress in the Andes and Himalayas. They found that natives in both highlands had faster basal metabolisms than lowlanders. They burned fat more quickly and had better circulation in their hands and feet. Both characteristics seemed to be adjustments to cold rather than to height, but cold is a year-round fact in high altitudes.

A fascinating study by Dr. I. G. Pawson considered the effects of high altitudes on the growth of children. He reported on children in the Andes and in Sherpa communities, on Tibetan refugees near Katmandu, and children living at high altitudes in Ethiopia. In all cases he found that the children, to some degree, were reduced in birth weight and grew more slowly. This retarded growth, he concluded at first, suggests environmental influence. But a more careful study that compared such people with their lowland cousins convinced him that genetic influence may be more important than anyone suspects.

Whatever it is that allows adaptation to high altitudes, whether it's genetic or environmental, it has taken place in natives who make the mountains their home. However, when these highlanders come down to the lowland, they experience a number of troubling symptoms. Their hearts slow down, and so does their metabolism. Overall they become less efficient, and more prone to catch infectious diseases.

What it all seems to indicate is that when you're used to one altitude and air pressure, it is difficult to adapt to substantially different altitude and air pressure. This may well explain why so many people feel discomfort and even become ill when fronts pass through. Fronts are accompanied by changes in air pressure. When the changes are rapid, we have no chance to grow accustomed to them. If we've been in a high-pressure system for days and suddenly it changes to a low-pressure system, we are in some ways like the lowlander who travels to the mountaintop in a few hours. We cannot adjust. Our entire system goes out of kilter, and we're literally left gasping for breath.

A quick change from a long-lasting low to a high is no better. We've become acclimated to the low pressure, and now all of a sudden it's high. We're like the highlander who comes down to the lowlands. There's more oxygen to breathe—too much oxygen—and we're not used to it. Our entire system has to readjust, and we go through all the problems readjustment brings.

We must also remember that cold air is denser than warm air. I realized that fact the first time when I was taken up in a hot-air balloon. The fabric of the balloon was stretched out on the ground of a sunny meadow, limp and empty. I watched as a burner was attached to the opening and the massive bag of nylon slowly filled and began to lift. When we climbed into the basket, it was straining at its ropes, a restless giant yearning to lift up into the blue. And yet it had nothing in it but air.

It pulled us up until the entire countryside was spread out below, and we hung there on the wind. To me, the most amazing thing about it all was that *air* was lifting into *air*. The air in the balloon was warmer than the outside air, and therefore it was thinner, and the balloon rose gently.

The cold, dense air outside the balloon had a higher barometric pressure than the light air inside. Had we risen to the point where the pressure inside equaled that outside, the balloon would have stopped and I would have had the same problem in breathing that our mountaineer had. As it was, the balloon didn't go that high. We drifted lazily at 5,000 feet, and I felt only a sense of exhilaration. Perhaps I breathed more quickly because of it, but I had no symptoms of oxygen starvation. Of course there should be none at that low altitude.

Consider the relative densities of cold and warm air in terms of air pressure. While the variation in pressure between fair weather and bad weather is about four times less than the variations between sea level and 13,000 feet, a low barometer means that the air contains less oxygen. It becomes harder to breathe, and perhaps this is one reason why so many heart problems occur when the barometer is low. The heart must work harder to feed our bodies the oxygen we need, and that hard work is an extra strain—not too much of a strain for a healthy person, but enough to send a cardiac case over the edge.

Dos and Don'ts

If you must move to Denver or another high area, and you're extremely weather sensitive, acclimate yourself gradually. Get up to the higher altitude in stages. Stop along the way and try to stretch your trip as long as you can.

If you are breathless in either mountain air or a low-pressure system, then increase your breathing rate. That will get more oxygen into your lungs and clear your head, but watch out that you don't get light-headed. You may be leaving too little carbon dioxide in your body.

If you live in the mountains and find that you're constantly short of breath, and that your blood pressure is high, see your doctor at once. If he finds that you have an elevated red blood cell count, you may have mountain sickness. In that case, get out of town fast and down to sea level.

If you are pregnant and have lived most of your life in the lowlands, try to avoid mountain climates until your child is born.

If you're weather sensitive and a skier, think twice about steep descents. You can ski down a high mountain in a short time and go from low pressure to high in minutes.

The other side of the altitude coin is the weather-sensitive mountain climber who ascends too quickly. Check your pulse as you go. It will rise as you exert yourself, but it shouldn't go any higher than 150. If it does, stop and rest till it slows down.

If you are over sixty or are a cardiac risk, if you have emphysema or any other lung problem, if you are a heavy smoker or live in a heavily polluted area, the following rules are important:

—Don't exert yourself when the air pressure is low. This is the time to settle down with a good book, stay warm, and if you want a drink by the fire, make it light.

—If you have to travel, avoid mountain areas. Cancel that walk or climb in the Alps, the train ride up the Andes, and if you must be in a mountainous area, don't try to keep up with the kids.

YOU *CAN* DO MORE ABOUT THE WEATHER THAN YOU THINK
Your Guides to Personal Daily Weather Modification

The principal purpose of these guides is to document the surprising variety of simple steps anyone can take to respond to the weather's language. Many of these suggestions are obvious indeed. Others may surprise you. Still others, not explicitly included here but applicable to your personal life routines, may occur to you after you examine these suggestions and the "Dos and Don'ts" listed throughout this book.

Key: Everyone □   Weather Sensitives ▨

Weather conditions	Clothing level	Work level	Daily pace	Immediate environment	Personal
Wet weather	Umbrellas, boots, or rubbers and rain hats. (Raincoats are better if made of artificial fibers. Avoid plastic.) Be sure your socks stay dry.	Keep in mind the physical dangers of outside work, driving in slippery conditions.	Drive as little as possible.	Keep yourself dry. If you must go out, dry off as soon as you come indoors.	Weather sensitives often react to rain with depression.
Humid weather	Wear loose clothing.	Avoid exertion if you work outdoors.	Be careful with household chores. Avoid using clothes drier, the oven, or doing heavy jobs.	Air conditioning is a big help. So is a good dehumidifier.	Be patient with your troubled feelings. Try to get out of town for a dry vacation. Watch children for their reactions to humidity.
Air-pressure fluctuations	Unimportant.	Avoid exertion when air pressure is low.	If you must move to a higher altitude, take the move in easy stages. Avoid going from high to low altitudes too quickly.	There is no way of changing your microclimate short of pressure chamber!	In high altitudes, or low-pressure periods, conserve your energy expenditure.

YOU CAN DO MORE ABOUT THE WEATHER THAN YOU THINK
Your Guides to Personal Daily Weather Modification

The principal purpose of these guides is to document the surprising variety of simple steps anyone can take to respond to the weather's language. Many of these suggestions are obvious indeed. Others may surprise you. Still others, not explicitly included here but applicable to your personal life routines, may occur to you after you examine these suggestions and the "Dos and Don'ts" listed throughout this book.

Key: Everyone ☐ Weather Sensitives ▨

Weather conditions	Clothing level	Work level	Daily pace	Immediate environment	Personal
Winds, hot and dry	Unimportant	Take extreme care if you do physical work or drive at work. Avoid legal and financial decisions.	Avoid exercise, physical exertion.	Stay indoors as much as possible. Consider a negative-ion generator if winds have a profound effect, but try it out first!	Try to avoid taking tests. Avoid emotional involvement.
When the fronts change	Unimportant	Try not to make any serious decisions during front activity or on day after front passes.	Watch relationships with others, friends, family, lover, colleagues.	If possible, try to relocate in a turbulent-free area.	If depression is a problem, ask your doctor for a mild mood-elevator. If you are troubled by sleeplessness, try relaxation exercises, milk at bedtime, or, failing these, a sedative.
Electrical and thunderstorms	Unimportant	Avoid driving and heavy physical work during thunderstorms.	Take things slowly during thunderstorms or heavy sunspot activity.	Try to find area that is ion-balanced or filled with negative ions. Avoid cities.	Remember: your judgment may be impaired during thunderstorms and sunspot activity.
Smog and air quality	Unimportant	Exertion, exercise, and sports can harm your lungs when air quality is poor.	Pace yourself slowly when air quality is poor.	Air conditioning will not help without sophisticated electronic filters.	If you have any breathing problem linked to poor air, try your best to change location.

YOU CAN DO MORE ABOUT THE WEATHER THAN YOU THINK
Your Guides to Personal Daily Weather Modification

The principal purpose of these guides is to document the surprising variety of simple steps anyone can take to respond to the weather's language. Many of these suggestions are obvious indeed. Others may surprise you. Still others, not explicitly included here but applicable to your personal life routines, may occur to you after you examine these suggestions and the "Dos and Don'ts" listed throughout this book.

Key: Everyone ▭   Weather Sensitives ▭

Weather conditions	Clothing level	Work level	Daily pace	Immediate environment	Personal
Hot weather	White or light-colored clothes. Thin, loose cotton; avoid artificial fibers. Try a parasol or umbrella. Avoid sun hats (they build up heat around your head).	Avoid overexertion. Make sure you get enough salt in your food.	Adapt to heat slowly. Avoid stressful exercise. If you must exercise, do it in cool of morning or early evening.	If you use air conditioning, keep temperature at 75°. A fan to circulate air is best. Take advantage of the shade.	Tan with care.
Cold weather	Layer your clothes. Try insulating underwear (wool is excellent insulator). Wear warm shoes and socks. Consider: hats, earmuffs, face masks.	When working or exercising outdoors, be careful not to breathe in too much cold air. A face mask may help. Cold exhaustion is as dangerous as heat exhaustion.	Adapt to the cold slowly. Avoid prolonged exposure.	Central heating is best, but keep it at no higher than 68°	If you do get frostbite, warm up with room-temperature water, never hotter than body heat.

Chapter Four

What Heat Really Does to You

Recently, in the comic strip "Doonesbury," Zonker was interviewed, on a radio talk show, as a tanning expert. "It takes a lot of discipline to achieve a truly competitive tan," he told the interviewer seriously, and added that he didn't turn pro earlier because he was disqualified for peeling.

Tanning in America and in parts of Europe is very close to a competitive sport. Certainly a good tan adds status to the tannee. In winter it hints of vacations in the tropics; in summer of long days at the beach or at some country club tennis court.

Never mind the broiling hours spent on city rooftops, in backyards, or under sunlamps—the effect is what counts, and there is a certain esthetic pleasure in a tanned skin. The more of your body you can tan, the better, although some white space is needed to show it's a tan, not natural skin color. The real pro sunbathes nude, no holds barred. The important thing, pro or amateur, is to avoid sunburn.

What is the difference between sunburn and suntan? Can

a tanned person be burned by the sun, or is his tan a protection? For that matter, is any dark skin a protection against the sun?

When I was a young man, I was at the beach one day with a black friend. We spread out a blanket and pulled off our pants. We were wearing bathing trunks under them, but my friend refused to take his shirt off.

"I get a mean sunburn," he told me.

"Sunburn? You?" I was bewildered, and he laughed at me. "Just because I'm dark-skinned doesn't mean I can't burn if I'm not careful."

He was right, of course. Skin color offers no total protection against sunburn. Skin is a complicated structure. There is a thin dead layer of cells on the outside, and this shields somewhat against the ultraviolet rays of the sun. These are the rays that really burn.

Under the dead layer of the skin, there is a living layer with blood vessels, sweat glands, and a pigment known as melanin. All of us—white, black, yellow, red, or brown—depend on the distribution of melanin in our skin to give us color. Unless you are albino, you have some of this pigment. It filters out some ultraviolet light, darkens in the process, and gives us a tan. People with a great deal of melanin, like my black friend, have a greater protection against the sun, but the protection is not complete. Some sun does get through. Too much sun and he can get sunburned.

Tanning is a complex process. If you go for a while without getting any sun, your pigment lightens and your tan fades; but get back in the sun and you will tan faster than a person just starting. The faded tan comes back but, unfortunately, this new tan won't protect you against burning. Your tan may take months, even years, to fade away, but the protection against sunburn that the tan gives fades in a few weeks.

Sunburn is different. Whereas tanning involves darkening of the pigment, in sunburn the skin (and blood vessels in it) have actually been burned.

Sometimes a bad case of sunburn can affect the entire body as seriously as a second-degree burn: this is *sun poisoning*. Finally, continual exposure to the sun, whether tanning or burning, always brings with it the danger of skin cancer.

Although a tan looks great on younger people, it is probably the worst thing an older person can do to the skin. The sun ages skin—dries it out and wrinkles it.

The Three Sources of Sunlight

I remember my first eclipse of the sun. I was about eight years old. My father carefully smoked a piece of glass by holding it over a candle. Looking through the sooty layer I saw the sun as a glowing ball in a murky sky. Slowly, as I watched, an edge of blackness ate into it. With a sudden chill in the summer air, the entire sun was gone and the earth, for a moment, hung in darkness.

"You must never look straight at the sun," my father warned me. "Not even in an eclipse. You'll go blind. You'll get eclipse blindness."

That was the first time I heard the phrase *eclipse blindness*. Later I found the term in a medical book and discovered that my father was right. The sun's fierce energy can burn the retina of the eye and damage the cells of the cornea. The damage can be temporary or, if you look at the sun too long, it can be permanent.

It doesn't take an eclipse or looking at the sun on a hot summer day to hurt your eyes. I had a cousin who was a good skier, but foolish. He went up and down the slopes throughout one bright sunny morning without goggles. By afternoon he was blind—snow blindness! Fortunately it didn't last. He just hadn't realized that the amount of sunlight that a field of snow reflects can be disabling and can cause blindness or severe sunburn.

Always remember there are three sources of sunlight during

a bright day. One is obvious—the direct light of the sun. Another is the light reflected from the sky, from either haze or dust particles. The third is the light reflected from the ground. Large expanses of snow will reflect a tremendous amount of sunlight, and so will desert sands, beaches, even city concrete.

Your Body's Wonderful Warning System

The troubling thing about exposure to sunlight is that we often do not realize how much heat we have taken in. We ignore our body's warning system, that feeling of fatigue and dizziness. We tell ourselves, "I'm just a little tired, but it's not *that* hot. If I just keep going, it'll pass." In fact, we are often the ones to pass instead of the symptoms.

A recent *New York Times* article told of two army recruits at Fort Jackson, South Carolina, who died of heat stroke after their first day of training. The weather was responsible. Ninety-nine degrees of heat led to cardiac arrest in two healthy and hardy seventeen-year-old men. They had been driven beyond the warning point. Their bodies said "stop" but everyone else was carrying on. They were either unaware that people differ in what they can tolerate, or else they ignored what their bodies were telling them. Each person's body warns of its limits and its ability to withstand extremes of weather. We must learn to listen to the warnings and interpret them.

One of the remarkable characteristics of the human body is that, within limits, it can adapt to unusual circumstances, even excess heat. In Victorian England the younger sons of the upper class were often shipped off to the colonies. When they left a temperate climate many could not adapt to the tropics. Their health and personality disintegrated.

Some, however, did manage to handle the heat. Unlike mad dogs, these particular Englishmen did not go out in the midday sun. They took up the native habit of a long rest at noon.

The secret of their adaptation to the tropics was taking the heat in small doses each day: mornings and late afternoons. Scientific studies have shown that people can manage two daily periods of heat, one or two hours each. Britishers who made the grade followed this pattern without the benefit of scientific studies.

In addition, they avoided overexertion, which isn't surprising. They had never been active at home. The British army private, the "Tommy," was able to work in the tropics because he was no stranger to physical exertion. But he too needed that same adaptation of two periods a day, morning and afternoon.

We can all adapt to tropical climates; the trick is to do it gradually. I remember a wonderful vacation I once took on a hot Caribbean island. I spent the first week lying in a beach chair under an umbrella watching a young accountant from Boston enjoy himself. He tried everything. He did waterskiing and skin diving, jogged along the beach, sailed a Sunfish, and at lunch he always had a dance or two with a pretty girl to the native band's music.

In three days he collapsed from exhaustion. The moral: If you sit on your butt at home, stay on it on vacation. If you want an active vacation, build up to activity before you leave home.

The body can cool off, but within limits. It does the job with three cooling systems. One is sweating. The evaporation of sweat cools our skin; the blood circulating in the capillaries near the skin is cooled in turn. In its turn, the blood cools the body. If we could go about without clothing, this system would work efficiently. The trouble is that clothing absorbs sweat and interferes with nature's cooling system. The use of deodorants that stop sweating interferes still further.

Breathing is a second, less efficient cooling system. We evaporate moisture through breathing and this helps cool us. That's one reason we pant when we exert ourselves in the heat.

The body's third cooling system is simply radiation. We

radiate heat from our skin to the air around us. For this to operate, the surrounding air must be cooler than our bodies. Shade and a breeze, even a warm breeze, will cool us quickly. In any case: Get out of the sun when overheated.

The first and best system, sweating, works well but unfortunately deprives us of essential body salts. I had a job one summer working in a construction gang. I was young and healthy and loved the work because it took me out of doors and I could sweat off excess energy.

I had a tan, and like the other men I discarded my shirt and worked stripped to the waist, the sweat pouring off me.

At the end of the first day, however, I was completely exhausted. I had to sit down for half an hour before I could go home. I had expected muscle aches, but this was too much! My head swam. I felt dizzy, sick to my stomach, and full of cramps.

"You sweated too much," a knowledgeable and friendly older worker told me. "You can't do that in this racket without getting sick."

"But I kept drinking water!"

"That's all the worse, sonny. Water is fine, but water and no salt thins out your blood. I tell you what. You get over to the boss. He's got some salt tablets. That'll fix you up."

He was right. If we sweat a lot we must replace the salt our bodies lose, as well as the water. We should also keep an eye on the body's potassium level. I managed that without realizing it because from then on I always had a large glass of orange juice in the morning and a banana for lunch. Oranges and bananas are both good sources of potassium.

Dos and Don'ts

"You kids will have to get your own dinner. I've been on my feet all day and they're killing me. They're all swollen and I'm holding water. It's too damn hot!"

Mother's trouble is *heat edema*. The solution: a mild diuretic. She should also sit down and elevate her feet. Most important, she should get out of the heat.

"I've run my two miles today but I'm just beat. It's really hot out there. I feel dizzy and I'm burning up!" Dad has staggered in from his running and he's lucky not to be delirious. The temperature is almost a hundred degrees and that insidious devil *water-depletion heat stress* has done him in.

The solution: a glass of water with a teaspoon of salt before he starts running and a glass afterwards. If his symptoms included nausea, vomiting, and cramps, his condition would be called *salt-depletion heat exhaustion*. I had a mild case of that on my construction job.

If dad had stretched his usual two-mile run to five and sweated up a storm, then taken three glasses of water when he finished, he might have had muscle cramps. These *heat cramps* would indicate a shift in his body's salt balance. The solution: potassium or magnesium pills to overcome the cramps. His family doctor will set him straight. In any case, if dad is going to run in hot weather he should discuss it with a doctor beforehand.

"I'm not a baby anymore but, Christ, when this hot weather sets in and I begin to sweat I get a rash all over." Johnny is sixteen and still has *prickly heat*. He sweats profusely and he's allergic to his own skin bacteria. A dermatological mess for Johnny; the solution is to stay cool. Use a light powder to absorb the sweat and keep the skin dry. He has to learn not to overexert himself in the heat.

"We had a hell of a volleyball game going at the beach. The guys against the gals, then guys and gals on each side; then Big Buck, he's the jock in the crowd, yells, 'I'm going to take you all on!' And bam! after five minutes he collapses right there on the sand, a big guy like that!" The bigger they are the harder they fall in the heat. Buck's blood went to his skin and away from his brain where it was needed, if only to let him think about taking it easy. Big Buck had *heat syncope*.

He was exhausted before he collapsed and giddy. He should have known enough to stop.

The solution: Don't overexert in the heat. If Big Buck had been able to keep going, as he wanted to, he might have gone on to *heat stroke* with a high fever, possible brain injury, and even death.

If you are really interested in tanning, do it gradually, and over a long period of time. If you are very fair-skinned, don't even try. If you have a moderate amount of pigment in your skin, don't stop and start the process again in a few weeks. Remember, your original tan of a week ago will not protect you as well as the tan of two days ago.

If you throw common sense to the winds and end up with a burn, try a moisturizing lotion instead of your usual remedy. It works well and it works quickly. If it's a bad burn, first take a cool bath with baking soda in it.

If neither of these remedies helps, take two aspirins with plenty of water. Aspirin decreases pain and shrinks swollen tissues. If the sunburn blisters—call your doctor.

Children should be warned about the danger of sun blindness. They should never look into the sun, especially during an eclipse. It's a treacherous time because the rays don't seem as harmful as they are.

Skiers should wear goggles, not only on sunny days, but also on overcast ones. Snow blindness heals itself in time, but the accidents it can cause may be serious.

A final warning about hot weather. Don't keep going because everyone else does, and don't try to finish that job if your body warns you to stop. Wait till evening to finish mowing the lawn, painting the house, or running that errand. Even if you are not weather sensitive to fronts and winds, you will be vulnerable to extreme heat. Everyone is, but most of us don't understand the weather language that our body speaks. Be weather-wise and listen.

Chapter Five

It's Not the Heat . . .

"Maybe you love New York," Natalie told her roommate, "but I can't stand it. I'm going back to Fargo."

Cal threw his hands up in despair. "I don't love New York —I endure it, especially in the summer. Back home in Tucson we had hot summers, God knows, but they were dry."

"Never mind the summer," Natalie said. "It's these winters I can't stand, cold and wet! No matter how cold Fargo was, it was never damp. I swear, if it weren't for our jobs . . ."

So goes the continuing argument between Natalie and Cal over the awful New York humidity. She wants to move back to Fargo, he wants to go to Tucson. The big problem is that, in terms of humidity, Cal is a summer sensitive. He doesn't mind the wet winters, but he crumples at the first humid summer day. On the other hand, Natalie can take the summer humidity "as long as I can shoot out to Fire Island on weekends." But she can't endure the bitter, wet winters. She's a winter sensitive.

Of the two, Cal's problem is more common. He really suffers when the THI goes up. "It's the worst feeling," he says. "I just can't describe it."

The THI that throws Cal into the doldrums was the brainchild of one of the men who worked for the United States Weather Bureau some time ago. He decided to find an exact and objective way of describing that "feeling" that so many people like Cal get when the humid summer begins.

He came up with the *Temperature Humidity Index* (THI). By a rather complicated calculation this is determined from the air temperature and the relative humidity. (Relative humidity is the amount of water in the air at any given temperature.)

The THI is a useful index of comfort, although it ignores wind and solar radiation. As a general rule, half of us are uncomfortable when the THI reaches 75; all are uncomfortable when it hits 80. Cal, however, went to pieces when it reached 60.

How Humidity Sensitive Are You?

There is no logical reason for Cal's reaction. A neighbor down the hall who has arthritis suffers when the humidity is high, and another neighbor with congestive heart disease is in trouble when the weather turns humid. But Cal is young and strong and healthy. His heart is in perfect shape, and he has no signs of arthritis. He is simply weather sensitive in a selective way. He can endure heat or cold and is rarely troubled by pollen or pollution. Highs and lows, fronts and ions have a minimal effect on him. But let the humidity rise just a bit and pow!—he's out of action.

Cal can't leave New York. His job opportunities there are too good. What finally saved his sanity, if not his health, was air conditioning. He would run the air conditioner in their apartment all through the summer, not for heat relief but to get rid of the humidity. Cal called air-conditioned cabs every day during the most humid weather to ride to his office and back. He worked in an air-conditioned building and refused to go to a restaurant or visit friends unless an air conditioner was going. "I lead an air-conditioned life," he told Natalie glumly, "and somehow I feel I'm missing out on something."

Cal's feeling may have had scientific validity. In Germany I talked to Dr. Volker Faust, a psychiatrist who has been very active in the field of biometeorology. He pointed out that while air conditioning is one solution for humidity-sensitive people, it is a solution with a price:

"What happens is that they fail to adapt. One of the most important elements in the way we handle the world around us is adaptation. If you cannot overcome a situation, you must adapt to it or suffer, and human beings are remarkably skillful at adaptation."

"But you're talking about psychological adaptation," I protested.

"Yes, but I include physical adaptation as well. We learn to adapt our bodies to cold. As a race, the Eskimos have done it. So have the Laplanders. We can adapt to heat. How many people live in hot desert areas? We adapt to altitude. We settle in the Andes and the Himalayas. My God, some day we may adapt to the ocean and live under water.

"But adaptation means experiencing the weather we adapt to. You don't adapt to humidity by continuously using air conditioners. If you do, when you get out of the air-conditioned house or car the humidity will seem twice as bad as it was before you got in."

"Then you advise stoical suffering?"

He grinned. "Within limits. I have air conditioning in this building. But it's a mental hospital." He shrugged. "The patients shouldn't have too hard a time adapting."

I think Dr. Faust's advice is fine for some people, but a summer sensitive like Cal who can't take any humidity must rely on air conditioning, and it can help many of us who are moderately humidity sensitive. There are just too many problems that excess humidity can cause.

In the course of writing this book, I interviewed hundreds of people to determine how many were weather sensitive and what aspects of the weather troubled them most. There are more humidity-sensitive women than men, and they seem to fall into a pattern. Shirley is a composite of all of those I talked to.

She is over thirty, not slim but not fat. She has about ten extra pounds tucked in here and there. She has a slight case of arthritis. Between her job and her children she is under a great deal of pressure. Shirley is a worrier and a hard worker.

"I know a humid day from the moment I wake up," she explains. "I can't see the humidity, but it's there. I could cut it with a knife. And I'm sleepy, just exhausted for the whole day. I feel so heavy, it's as though the atmosphere weighed me down. I have no energy, and yet I know I have to get things done."

That tired, lethargic feeling is what you hear about when you discuss humidity with these sufferers. "The worst thing about humidity," another woman told me, "is being married to someone who isn't bothered by it. You have no idea how bad you feel when your husband is bright and eager and full of life and you're just dragging around. You seem twice as tired yourself, twice as heavy."

What happens, she said, is that inevitably the humidity sensitive who is married to a nonsensitive begins to think that her suffering is all in her head. "You think you feel miserable with no good reason. You're sure something is wrong with you. You become shrink material."

This attitude, incidentally, is typical of many weather-sensitve people, no matter what aspect of the weather they're sensitive to. It's particularly true when they are married to a nonsensitive, or when they are the only weather sensitive in a family. They begin to doubt their own symptoms. Too often, their doctor, unaware of the impact of weather on health, will put these people down as hypochondriacs or chronic complainers.

But the complaints are justified; enough studies prove that. One investigator showed that in Denver, when the weather was humid, children in school had to be disciplined five times as often as in dry weather. Another study checked public libraries in a number of cities and discovered that people took out "serious" books when the weather was dry and "light" books when it was humid.

Still another study proved that humid weather caused men and women to become gloomy, sullen, and irritable. But these are all traits we can live with. Far more disturbing events can take place in hot and humid weather.

In India, in the 1920s and 1930s, one-third of all religious riots took place in humid weather. Not so disturbing and nearer to home, a study of 40,000 arrests in New York City showed that while the heat of early summer caused crime to peak, the humidity of August caused it to fall off. Even criminals were too drained of energy to work hard.

Humans are not the only ones influenced by humidity. It hits the animal world as well. Dogs and cows sense growing humidity in the air, and they react to it with growing restlessness. Even the lowly flea reacts. A study in Vietnam in the early 1970s showed that high humidity may limit the plague in man because in some way it slows up the fleas that spread it.

Another study of peptic ulcers concluded that humidity plays an important role in whether or not they perforate. When the humidity is high and the temperature is also high, the number of perforated peptic ulcers increases.

All these studies are based on statistics and observations. The reactions of people to humidity are so varied that it is difficult to take physiological measurements that would show how we manage this type of weather.

Dr. Tromp in Holland points to two studies that examined the physical reactions of people exposed to high and low humidities. By comparing the subjective reactions (what these people felt) with the objective findings (what really happened), the researchers hoped to understand why people react the way they do to humidity.

The experiments unfortunately gave contradictory results. In one, humidity had no effect on how the people felt, and in the other when the humidity was low they complained of feeling cold.

These experiments were not well controlled and only included a small number of subjects, but I think their real failure lay in the fact that there is such a variation in the way people experience humidity. One person's comfort zone is another person's hell. On top of this, no biological reason has been found for why we "sense" humidity.

Dr. Tromp writes, "It is known that air humidity, as such, cannot be discerned by the human body." He goes on to say that we can only feel the difference between high and low humidities.

When we are too hot, nature cools us off by letting us sweat. The evaporation of the sweat is a cooling process. High humidity allows less of our sweat to evaporate.

In cold, humid weather, the discomfort of humidity sensitives may be due to the fact that their skin absorbs water vapor from the humid air around them.

Clothes too absorb water and become moist when we are outdoors in humid weather, and this adds to our discomfort.

There are still many unexplored areas in the study of sensitivity to humidity. Much more research has to be done before scientists can measure and explain the discomfort of this kind of weather. Weather-sensitive people know it is uncomfortable, even painful, because they can feel it, and even those of us who are only slightly sensitive squirm on a heavily humid day.

Dos and Don'ts

In humid weather, wear loose clothes.

Make allowances for yourself and realize that you are weather sensitive. On a bad day, indulge your miserable feelings. Sometimes just getting it all out helps.

Use air conditioning sparingly to avoid reentry shock, but do use it when the humidity soars.

Try climate therapy—a vacation in a dry, nonhumid place—if you possibly can.

Don't bake a cake, work on your car's motor, scrub the floors, or put clothes in the dryer when the humidity is high. The dryer just adds more moisture to the air. The baking adds heat, which makes the humidity harder to stand, and the other jobs make you sweat; and in humid weather sweat is just another problem. Stay cool with shade and fans.

If you are a weather sensitive and involved in an intimate relationship with another weather sensitive, work out some ground rules about your individual reactions. Understanding your partner's feelings on a hot, humid day makes him or her easier to live with.

Parents should watch the way their children react to heat and humidity. Older people and children are particularly sensitive. Older people can complain about the weather—and they do—but very young children can't put it into words.

Chapter Six

What the Cold Does to You

In 1977 a woman was found in a back alley of a large city during the dead of winter. She was wearing only a light house-dress and had been drinking heavily. When the ambulance came for her, the attendants were sure she was dead. Her skin was as cold as ice; she was pale and her lips were blue.

"She looked like a marble statue," the ambulance attendant told a newspaper reporter. "Maybe not so pretty, but just as stiff. Her eyeballs—man! They were like glass!"

To everyone's amazement, the woman was still alive and had a faint, cold breath. Her pulse varied from 12 to 20, and she was down to three or four breaths a minute. Her body temperature was only 64° Fahrenheit, yet she was living and, miraculously, she survived. Miraculously, because humans are frail creatures. We are only comfortable in a narrow range of internal body temperatures that hover around 98° Fahrenheit. If our temperature rises to 108° or 110°, we lose consciousness and go into convulsions. We may even die. At temperatures below 90° we also lose consciousness, but we don't necessarily die.

There have been many cases of survival in extreme cold. People who were lost in snowstorms and half frozen to death, and others who were saved from shipwrecks after long hours in freezing water, have lived to tell their stories.

In surgery, particularly open-heart surgery, lowering the body temperature (hypothermia) used to be a very useful technique, although recently it has fallen into disfavor. Many years ago I witnessed an operation on a young man with a defective heart valve in which cooling was an essential part of the procedure.

I still remember the sterile whiteness of the room, and the blazing lights, the green gowns and masks of the surgical team, and the waxy pallor of the young man. His chest was opened and the blood was pumped through a circuit that would return it to his body while the surgeons operated. En route the blood was cooled, which in turn cooled the heart. When it stopped beating, the heart was taken out of the circuit and the surgeons worked on the cold organ.

Later, when I asked the surgeons why the heart had to be cooled, they explained that the heart's temperature, when it stopped beating, was 55°. At that low temperature there is little if any bleeding, and the surgical repair can be clean and swift. Most important, the tissue is not damaged, and when they warm it up, the heart starts beating again.

That low a temperature, of course, is never reached by any body organ except in such unusual circumstances. It is much too low for survival. Yet curiously enough, when I asked a physiologist about that, he said, "The low temperature itself doesn't cause death. It makes us stop breathing, and that's what does us in. Get your lungs to start again and you can survive."

All the recent interest in cryogenics (preserving a body indefinitely through freezing) has made one thing clear. Without an elaborate heart-lung machine setup, it would be impossible to get a person below 50° and still keep him or her alive, nor have we learned how to preserve the frozen body cells or, afterwards, to defrost them.

How You Can Adapt to Cold

In normal circumstances, civilized man can tolerate only a limited amount of cold if he expects to survive, but primitive man learned to live with cold.

When Charles Darwin sailed around the world on the *Beagle* and landed at Tierra del Fuego, the southernmost tip of South America—a barren, cold, inhospitable land—he was amazed to find Indians living there. Not only were they living there but, as he wrote in a letter home, "In this wretched climate subject to such extreme cold, is it not wonderful that human beings should be able to exist unclothed and without shelter?"

This "wretched climate" went down to 53° on some days, yet the Indians of Tierra del Fuego were able to adjust to it with neither clothes nor houses. This is not an isolated case. The Australian aborigines live in the same type of cold at night. They sleep around fires, it's true, but without clothing or shelter. But they are born into this environment. We depend on central heating and warm clothes and we couldn't survive in temperatures of 50° or 60° without them.

However, we can learn to adapt to even lower temperatures if we have protective clothing and we learn one simple technique. My wife, who grew up in Minneapolis, calls it the "toe-in-the-water factor."

"When I go swimming in cold water, I dip in a toe, then pull back—go a bit further in, then pull back. In the same way, when I was a kid, I went out in the cold in short spurts.

"Minneapolis is one cold city and I lived downtown. I'd go out and walk for five minutes, until I was pretty near frozen, then I would go into a store and browse around for five minutes until I warmed up. Then out into the cold again. I'd do that five or six times. I was then able to take the cold for the rest of the day. I would finally be able to play outside without my teeth chattering."

Not everyone is as sensible as my wife. Some people try to defy the cold. During World War II a group of Anzacs—Australian–New Zealand troops—were stationed in Camp Myles Standish in Massachusetts. It was a cold New England winter, and the American soldiers were bundled up against the cold. Those were days when they thanked Providence for those aunts back home who knitted heavy mufflers and gloves.

Not the Anzacs. They had their status to uphold. They weren't going to give in to foolish American customs. They wore their shorts and knee socks, their broad-brimmed hats, and their shirts open to expose their rugged chests. And at the station hospital there was a steady stream of frostbite patients. The American medical corps could not get through to them the simple equation that freezing weather and exposed skin equals frostbite.

It always started as a simple burning sensation or a stinging and itching, and that was easy for the Anzacs to ignore. The next stage was numbness, and that didn't hurt either. It was only the following day when the "bitten" areas turned red and blistered that our allies would come shambling over to the hospital: "Hey, Yank, you gotta do something to help me."

Understanding Cold-Weather Language

Another deceptively dangerous result of cold injury is what the army used to call *trench foot*. The soldiers who had to spend days with wet feet in cold, wet trenches during World War I developed numb, swollen feet and legs. This would be followed by leg cramps, pain, blistering of the skin, ulcers, and eventually, if nothing was done, by gangrene.

Trench foot is not only a casualty of war. It can happen to hikers who go through cold, wet places without stopping to dry their feet and change their socks. It can happen to anyone exposed to rain and cold for long periods. Usually the person who gets trench foot isn't aware that it's happening. It is only after days of wearing the same shoes and socks, wet and cold, that he takes them off and realizes that his feet hurt like hell.

Extreme cold warns us of the damage it can do. It speaks a very obvious weather language, but too often we ignore it. Carolyn, a suburban mother, whose life centered on her kids and her home, never imagined she'd have any damaging experience with cold. She was aware of heat exhaustion and took care that her family was protected in the summer, but she didn't realize that cold exhaustion is a killer, too. When it gets too cold outside, our body mechanism can fail us.

"Last year during that big snowstorm, I was on my way to pick up the kids at school. I was worried about them, so I took a shortcut on a back road," Carolyn told me. "You know, our place is back in the hills, and by the time I had driven a few miles, the wind was blowing fiercely and the snow was drifting.

"Of course I got stuck and couldn't get out of one of those drifts. I managed to get the car door open, and I started walking. I was just wearing a driving coat, but I figured it was less than a mile back to the main road, and it was. After a few minutes I was exhausted. I kept pushing on, but I was so tired. All I wanted to do was lie down in the snow and sleep.

"Once I stumbled and just lay there, but I made myself get up. Luckily, a local farmer was out with his snowplow looking for stranded motorists and he found me. I know I could never have made it to the crossroads, or even back to my car!"

Carolyn was right. She couldn't have gone on because she was suffering from cold exhaustion. As her body temperature dropped, she found it hard to breathe. Her heart began to slow down, and her entire body was oxygen-starved. It was harder and harder for Carolyn to move. At one point, the final solution seemed sleep, which would have been final.

Carolyn should have been warned as soon as she left the car that the cold was more than she could take. She told me that she "shivered at first and got goose bumps, but I just ignored them. I felt I had to get out of there."

Shivering is one of the body's defenses against the cold; "goose bumps" is another. When we shiver, the muscular action of the trembling skin brings on some local warmth. Goose bumps occur when the skin bunches up to become thick and less likely to lose heat.

Neither works well in the extreme cold that Carolyn faced. A number of other internal defenses do help, however. We can increase our metabolic rate, burning up body fat faster to create more heat, or we can constrict the capillaries near the skin. This means less blood flow on the surface and therefore less cooling of the bloodstream. Sometimes, paradoxically, the body opens up those surface capillaries to warm the skin with the blood.

All this automatic work is done by the hypothalamus, and some researchers have concluded that a psychological element exists in cold adaptation. "Thinking warm will help you keep warm," they insist. "People who expect to be cold will usually live up to that expectation, whereas people who are determined that the cold won't affect them will often be able to endure extreme cold with little discomfort."

Dos and Don'ts

When you shiver or get goose bumps or chills, nature is using weather language to warn you either to dress more warmly or get out of the cold. If you disregard these warnings, you can be in trouble. You may end up with painful, even dangerous, injuries. When your arms or feet are cold too long, the same closing off of circulation used by your body to protect itself can begin to starve the tissues. Your feet and hands may not get enough blood.

Chilblains is an old-fashioned term for a mild cold injury. When you get chilblains, your hands, feet, and ears itch and hurt. Being out too long in cold, damp weather causes it. Solutions: earmuffs, a face mask, warm mittens, and good, warm socks with waterproof boots.

If your circulation is poor to begin with or if your exposure to cold weather is too long and there is a stiff wind, you can get *frostbite*. When this happens, the tissue is actually frozen. Frostbite hits the most vulnerable and exposed parts of the body: hands, feet, ears, nose, and cheeks.

The solution? Doing something about it isn't simple once frostbite has taken place. It's much easier to take precautions and prevent it. Don't wait to seek shelter until you're uncomfortably cold. Cover all exposed parts of your body. If there's a wind, remember the wind-chill factor. It can lower the temperature tremendously.

It doesn't take long to get frostbite, so don't stay out long in frigid weather unless you absolutely must, and watch children. Their ideas of time are often vague. In spite of parental warnings, an incredible number of children suffer from frostbite each year.

If, in spite of all these warnings, you do end up with frostbitten ears, nose, or fingers, *don't* rub them with snow or put them in ice water. Old superstitions die slowly, and these are particularly persistent. Warm your fingers or cheeks slowly, starting with water at room temperature and never higher than your body heat.

Once the skin is damaged by frostbite, it is very easy to damage it further. You become insensitive to burning, and then insult can be added to injury.

When you treat frostbite, it is important to warm your entire body, not just the frostbitten area. The blood circulating in your warm body will defrost the damaged tissue from the inside as you warm it from the outside.

Don't massage the frostbitten area. Avoid possible damage to the skin. Be scrupulously clean so that no infection can take place. Tissue resistance will be low.

If you follow these rules, your chance for recovery without losing an ear, a nose, or a finger is excellent.

Trench foot: The solution is simple. Dry your feet and change your socks every day in rainy or cold weather as soon as they get damp. Don't go around with cold, wet feet. If you're out hiking in the cold, don't keep going after you've stepped in a big puddle. Stop, dry off, and put on that extra pale with black-and-blue areas, get to a doctor fast!

If, in spite of all warnings, you've been in wet socks and shoes all day and your feet, after you dry them, are cold and pale with black and blue areas, get to a doctor fast!

Cold exhaustion: Carolyn was wearing a light jacket when she was threatened by cold exhaustion. She felt that she didn't need anything more while driving in a heated car, no matter how cold it was outside. Proper clothes could have helped her —once her car got stuck. Cold-weather clothes should be made of material that lets perspiration out and lets air in.

Pockets of trapped air in clothes are great insulators. Socks should be heavy, but they too should trap air. Had Carolyn been properly dressed, she would have stood a better chance of reaching the main road on foot. However, in the bitterly cold weather, with drifting snow and a blowing wind, the odds were against her. Like many people, she underestimated the awesome power of a snowstorm.

Chapter Seven

Body Types, Clothing, and Personality

Sean is a long, skinny drink of water, six feet tall and not much more than 110 pounds. His nicknames vary from "The Anorectic Kid" to "Skeleton Man," and Sean takes them all with shy good nature. It's hard to believe that he has the strength to stand up, much less walk, but a few years ago, during a hot summer day, a group of us decided to take a hike down the Connecticut River. It was a foolish decision because the heat was just too much for us. One by one we dropped out to rest in the shade of bushes and trees along the riverbank.

Finally only Sean was left, and he completed the hike with no apparent discomfort. Later I said, "I don't know how you can stand heat like that."

"Heat doesn't bother me," Sean shrugged, "but I come apart in the winter. I just can't take the cold."

I couldn't understand Sean's surprising tolerance to heat until my daughter, studying for an anthropology test, set me straight. "It's a matter of body build, dad. Sean is tall and thin, like some of the African people who live in the desert heat. Did you know that the Dinka tribesmen are tall, but average only about ninety pounds?"

"I didn't know that, but what has that got to do with Sean's heat tolerance?"

"Someone who is thin and has long arms and legs has a greater body surface in proportion to their mass. They dissipate heat more efficiently because they have more skin, just the way the short, stocky Eskimos have less skin and lose less heat." She looked at me with a grin. "Didn't I teach you properly?"

I laughed, but when I saw Sean again I noticed that he was extraordinarily long-legged and his arms had a simian swing to them. He was white-skinned, but he certainly had the body build of a tall, thin African tribesman.

W Types and K Types

I was reminded of my daughter's anthropology lesson recently while browsing through some research on man's resistance to weather. According to Dr. M. Curry, in a publication of the American Bioclimatic Research Institute, man's ability to resist heat and cold is related to his body build.

Dr. Curry divides people into two groups: the *cold-front people*, whom he labels K types, and the *warm-front people*, whom he calls W types. The K types, according to Dr. Curry, are introverts—withdrawn, quiet, tall, and thin, with long arms and legs and a narrow face. They are weather sensitives, particularly reactive to cold air and the passage of cold fronts.

The W types are extroverts, fun-loving and outgoing. They are shorter, fatter, with round faces and stocky builds. They are also weather sensitives, but particularly to warm weather, warm fronts, and hot tropical air.

It might be fun to go through history and see who was a W and who a K, and how they reacted to weather and the world.

Certainly Abe Lincoln was a K type. He was tall and rangy, introverted, and unable to bear the cold (remember that constant wool shawl?).

Napoleon—outgoing, aggressive, and roly-poly in build—had no fear of invading winter-bound Russia. Cold didn't faze him, even if the invasion was a dreadful mistake. He seems a likely W type.

You can play the same weather game with your friends. Match their builds against their weather tolerance and see how close you come. If you find that you yourself illustrate one of these two body types, check your own weather resistance. Most people are in the middle—average in build and average in toleration of heat and cold.

Once we have found both W and K types, is there anything else we can tell about them? Dr. Curry labeled them introvert and extrovert, and if his labels fit, then there should be such a thing as a weather personality.

In Germany, when I talked to Dr. Faust, the psychiatrist and biometeorologist, he was certain that the concept is sound. He felt that the person who was emotionally volatile, whose moods went up and down, was also a weather-sensitive personality. But he didn't go as far as Dr. Curry and divide them into hot and cold sensitives. Dr. Faust believes a weather-sensitive personality is affected by all weathers—and I think that an additional implication exists. The weather sensitivity may well cause the moodiness.

A number of other researchers have found a complex relationship between personality and weather sensitivity. In 1958 two army doctors tested seventy enlisted men. The idea was to see how each personality type endured different weather elements. The men were first given the Psychological Personality Inventory Tests to classify the personality of each one.

The army had a number of climate chambers available, rooms in which the heat, humidity, and even the wind pattern could be controlled to simulate a broad variety of weather conditions. The men, stripped to their shorts for the experiment, stretched out for thirty minutes in a room with a 70° temperature, a 50 percent relative humidity, and a 5-mile-an-hour wind.

They were monitored carefully. Their objective reaction was measured by body temperature; their subjective reactions were obtained by questionnaires. The results in some cases were inconclusive, and in others remarkable. No matter what the psychological makeup, each man's body went down to the same temperature during the test. But all those with unusual personalities—highly introverted, extroverted, or neurotic—took much longer times for their body temperatures to return to normal after the test. The researchers had expected that different personalities would result in different body temperatures when the men were exposed to cold.

When the men were questioned about how cold they felt, the researchers expected that the different personality types would feel the weather differently, that neurotics would be much more weather sensitive than stable personalities. But the tests showed no such differentiation.

The results *did*, however, agree with those of the earlier work of Dr. Curry. There was a difference in weather sensitivity *according to body build*. Heavy, compact men felt warmer during this cold test than lightweight men. The two types of responses resembled Curry's type K and type W, at least in overall body area. The lightweight men may not have been as tall as Curry's Ks, but their amount of body skin was greater than that of the compact men. Like the Ks, they couldn't endure the cold as well as the heavier men. It would be interesting to know the results if the army had carried this experiment further and tested the men for heat sensitivity as well as for cold.

To find out more about cold perception, another experiment was designed to learn whether, when the air is damp, people feel colder in cold weather. Six comfortably dressed people were asked to walk half a mile outdoors in the winter;

humidity and temperature were measured while they walked.

It was a cold day with an overcast sky, but with low humidity. Nevertheless, all the subjects complained of dampness. The overcast sky was enough to make them feel that it was also humid.

When the six walkers were carefully questioned, however, the investigators found that relative humidity does affect perception of temperature but not in the way that had been expected. They had assumed the walkers would find it colder if they thought it was humid. Actually, they felt it was warmer than it in fact was. Two factors influenced their perception: They perceived the weather as damper than it was because the sky was overcast, and warmer than it was because they thought it was damp.

How we perceive heat or cold, and how we endure it, is also related to our adaptation to each, and sometimes to the way our bodies interpret the difference between hot and cold. For example: For most people a temperature of 75° is uncomfortably warm during the winter, but it may seem pleasant in summer. All we need is a hot spell of 85° or 90°, and a house with a temperature of 75° will feel comfortable, even cool.

In the summer, when the air temperature is 75°, we may become so used to it that if we step into an air-cooled store at 70° we will feel chilled.

Clothing Can Do More Than You Think

It has long been accepted that women are more cold sensitive than men. (I know a man who tells me that he and his wife go through a laughable routine, his wife putting the thermostat up every time she passes it, and he turning it down when he passes.)

Two enterprising researchers set out to test this theory by dressing a group of women in men's clothes and a group of men in women's clothes and letting them move around at winter temperatures. The experimental transvestites were questioned about their weather sensitivity a few days later, and their weather sensitivity was reversed, just as their clothes were!

The men who had been able to take a good deal of cold without shivering were now constantly cold, and the women who had not been able to tolerate the cold in their dresses took it very well in men's heavy suits. The difference, according to the experts, appeared to be primarily due to the clothes men and women wore, but this experiment was carried out in 1941. Today there is less difference in weight between the clothes of men and women. Women are quite at home in pants, and although men have yet to take to skirts, contemporary studies indicate that women are still more sensitive to cold than men.

To set myself straight on clothes and weather sensitivity, I went to New Haven, Connecticut, to visit Dr. Jan A. J. Stolwijk, associate director of the Pierce Laboratory, and a professor at Yale's Department of Epidemiology and Public Health. The John B. Pierce Foundation Laboratory is known around the world for its studies on how people adjust to hot and cold, its research on air pollution, on the sensations of smell and taste, and on the mechanisms of fever.

The foundation has a number of climate-controlled rooms, and, with Dr. Stolwijk, I watched healthy young Yale student volunteers exercise on stationary bicycles while their skin temperatures, heart rate, blood flow, respiration, and perspiration were charted and analyzed.

"What we study here," Dr. Stolwijk told me, "is how the different systems of the body work under every type of weather condition."

"What have you found out?" I asked, impressed at the enormous amount of energy being expended in the rooms.

"For one thing, whatever the weather stress, the person who

is physically fit can handle it better than the person who is out of condition."

Back in his office, I asked Dr. Stolwijk about battling the heat. "I've heard other biometeorologists knock air conditioning on the grounds of adaptation. They say it doesn't allow the body to adapt to the heat. What do you think?"

He nodded. "I agree with them, and I'd like to put in a plug for the old-fashioned fan. I feel it is far better to move the air around than to cool it off. In my opinion, there is nothing as good as the southern ceiling fans, the kind you see in old New Orleans. A gentle air motion downward can be a big help.

"In hot weather, the most important tip I can give you about being comfortable is stay out of the sun. I know that sounds obvious, but many people forget it, and they forget, too, that there is an enormous difference between sun and shade. In the sun the effective air temperature can be ten degrees higher than the actual temperature."

I nodded. "I can see that. I always feel cooler under a tree. They must be nature's air conditioners."

"They are. The leafy tree is shade on shade, air trapped between layers of leaves. It insulates the ground below."

What the Clo Factor Means

"What about clothes?" I asked. "Is there any special way you should dress in the heat?"

"Yes. White or light-colored clothes make a big difference. They reflect solar radiation. Dark clothes absorb it. You can heat a swimming pool, you know, by painting it black. It will absorb enough light from the sun to warm the water. Wear a black suit or dress on a hot day, and you'll get hotter and hotter.

"It's amazing how little people know about clothes. Here

in this institute clothes are an essential part of our study. Back before we got into World War I, one of our scientists, Dr. Gagge, worked on the insulating quality of clothes. He devised the *clo*, a way of measuring the ability of clothes to keep heat in or out."

"What is a clo?"

"Basically, it's a unit of insulation. A clo value of 1.0 was arbitrarily assigned to the insulating value of the average man's business suit back in nineteen forty-one—it was heavier then than it is now. A pair of warm twill slacks would be .44 clo and something as skimpy as a bikini is only .15 clo."

"But what use are these measurements?"

"Well, they're useful to set a series of standards. We can plan what someone should wear under any conditions. A lot of government agencies use the standards. NASA, for instance, uses them in suiting up the astronauts."

"But what about your average man or woman? What advice would you give them on dress?"

He smiled. "Some basics: When it's cold, layer your clothes. Layered clothes trap air between the layers, and they raise the clo value. They prevent body heat from escaping, and you can take some of the layers off when you go from very cold to slightly cold or even warm."

"And in the heat?"

"I told you about black and white. But avoid layering in hot weather. Wear thin, loose clothes that let air through. Remember, you want your sweat to evaporate and air to come in."

"You talked about the layered look. It's in style now. Do you think style reflects people's needs in clothes?"

"Not often. We dress for fashion instead of comfort and health, and we keep our house heat too high. Thermostats should be set at sixty-five or sixty-eight degrees and we should dress *up* to be comfortable at that temperature. Style won't let us, but it would be healthier if we could do it."

"I was in the city this summer," I told Dr. Stolwijk, "and

it was close to a hundred degrees, yet I saw many women wearing the 'Annie Hall look'—you know, a shirt with a vest over it, and a tie. It seemed a lot of clothes just for style."

"I agree. It sounds like too much for hot summer weather. I also think that women dress much too lightly when the weather turns cold. It's strange that this is so, because women tend to feel the cold more than men do. The weather gives them a message, but often they don't listen to it."

"Maybe they don't speak weather language."

"Indeed they don't! For one thing, hot weather tells them to sweat. Hot weather tells all of us to sweat, and sweat is a good thing for the body. By evaporating, it cools us. But sweat has become an unfashionable word. We've forgotten how to sweat, and we have to relearn how."

"Why is humid hot weather more uncomfortable than dry hot weather?"

"When the air is wet, the sweat doesn't evaporate, and we're uncomfortably damp. When the air is dry, it evaporates faster and cools us off." He frowned a bit, and then said, "There's a good deal of confusion going around about humidity. We hear that there is a high humidity, and we begin to feel rotten. But humidity is associated with temperature.

"You can have a relative humidity of one hundred percent and a temperature of eighty-five degrees and you won't be able to cool your skin at all. You can't evaporate sweat into that kind of hot, humid air.

"But you can have the same hundred percent humidity with a temperature of only sixty degrees, and you can sweat comfortably because the temperature of your skin is ninety-five degrees, higher than the temperature of the air around you.

"And at a still lower temperature, say a winter cold of zero degrees with a relative humidity of one hundred percent, the air will cause your skin to dry out so much that you will chap. What really affects us is the combination of temperature and humidity, not humidity alone."

What Fibers Protect You Best

Stella, a woman in her sixties, recently told me of an embarrassing problem. "You can write about it, but don't use my real name. I'm too shy about these things. The point is, ever since my menopause I've had hot flushes, times when I break out into a full sweat. I never sweated much before. I still don't, even in hot weather, unless I'm having a 'flush.'"

"That's pretty normal," I reassured her.

"I know. And the doctor told me my flushes would get fewer as I got older—a lot he knows. But the point is, I'll put on my nightgown—I have some very beautiful nylon ones that feel as light as silk—and I'll fall asleep very comfortably. Then I'll wake in the middle of the night after a flush, cold and clammy. It's just irritating."

"Have you tried sleeping in the raw?"

She smiled. "I'm basically an old-fashioned woman, and my husband is almost seventy. I don't think he could take the shock. But seriously, why should that happen? Is it the nylon? That's what my husband thinks, but I'd hate to give the nightgowns up."

Her husband was right, as I learned from the work of Dr. E. T. Renbourn. Dr. Renbourn is a physiologist who investigated clothing and equipment for the War Office in Great Britain. He notes that while synthetic fibers have certain advantages—they are shrinkproof, crease resistant, absorb little water, and dry quickly—they also have disadvantages. "Their low water uptake gives them a high degree of annoying static electricity."

Some biometeorologists who are advocates of *ion therapy* feel that this may be an advantage, especially to arthritis sufferers. The static charge in their clothes may contain enough ions to help the arthritic. But there is no scientific foundation for this idea.

Dr. Renbourn's major criticism of artificial fibers in clothing is their inability to take up water, the same reason that they dry quickly. Natural fibers—cotton, wool, linen—can absorb a great deal of water. Cotton can take up 20 percent of its weight, and wool 40 percent. When we sweat, natural-fiber cloth takes up the sweat. Artificial fibers do not, and we stay wet and uncomfortable.

The reason Stella's hot flush left her with a damp, clammy feeling was that those beautiful nylon nightgowns did not absorb her sweat. She would have been better off with a cotton nightgown.

The lesson is: Cotton sleepwear and underwear is best for men and women in urban and suburban living. It absorbs sweat.

Wool absorbs sweat too, and it's a better insulator than cotton. It's better for rugged outdoor living in cold weather. Old-fashioned woolen long johns were a good idea.

Synthetic underwear may be easier to care for and cheaper than cotton or wool, but it won't absorb sweat and can create damp areas in skin folds. These can become breeding places for bacteria and infection.

Dr. Renbourn suggests that rain clothes be made of synthetic fiber, since natural fibers take up moisture and become heavy, losing their insulating ability along with the trapped air inside their weave. The synthetics repel water and dry quickly. Rubberized or plasticized cloth, or plastic rain clothes, are not good because there's no way the body sweat can escape. Wearing them, we become encased in a miniature steam bath.

As for wind protection, this depends less on the type of fiber than on the type of weave. Tight weaves close up the air spaces and protect the wearer more.

Dr. Renbourn is not as certain as Dr. Stolwijk of the benefit of white over dark clothes in the sun. "Textiles are not continuous surfaces, and the heat that isn't reflected away by the outer fibers may be reflected back to the body."

As an indication that nature may be ahead of man in this

matter, he notes that many furry animals have long white hairs and short black hairs under them. The white hairs reflect the light, protecting the animal against too much heat, while the black hairs underneath absorb whatever light gets through, protecting the skin.

I think the final word on this reflection business was the advice of a friend, Paul, who spends his summer vacation in a nudist camp. "I am of the white racial persuasion," he said jokingly. "I'm better off in hot weather running around bare-assed than wearing any kind of clothes. I'm not hairy, and my skin reflects half the sun's heat. That's not all. A breeze on my fair body peps up my muscle tone. That's a little-known scientific fact. It's why you feel so good without clothes on."

"What about sunburn?" I asked.

"Oh, well, I don't burn. I tan and I do it gradually. It cuts down on the amount of heat I reflect, I will admit, but on the other hand, I become adapted to the heat by the time I've gotten my tan."

Some scientific basis for Paul's nudist feeling can be found in Dr. E. F. Adolph's book *Physiology of Man in the Desert*. In it he talks of trials under desert conditions when nude men encountered difficulties. They sweated more while they were nude and needed more drinking water. But he doesn't go as far as Paul in advocating nudity. He advises wearing loose, billowing clothes like the desert Arab's.

"They act as a tent to absorb heat at a distance from the body." As a curious contradiction to the reflective ability of white cloth, he notes that the clothes of the wealthier Arabs are usually dark, as are the dresses of the Arab women. The reason probably is social or religious custom, or the unavailability of white cloth rather than any thought of protection from the sun. Certainly the dark fabrics absorb more heat.

In fact, all over the world the clothes that people wear are based not so much on attempts to come to grips with the weather as on tradition, what's available, and religious and social customs—and of course on fashion. As Dr. Stolwijk told me, "Fashion is the great enemy of common sense in all climates. When the chips are down, given a choice between what is best for the wearer and what is in fashion, human beings will almost always choose fashion."

Dos and Don'ts

Wind is the biggest enemy in the cold weather. It blows away the insulating layer of air that keeps us warm. The wind-chill factor can cause us to freeze no matter how bearable the temperature might seem. At 20°, in a 20-mile-an-hour wind, the cooling effect is equal to calm air at −10°.

The clothes that will keep you warm at 70° if you remain still will keep you warm at 40° if you walk briskly and at −5° if you run.

Moisture increases the loss of body heat. Water is a better conductor of heat than air; therefore, if your skin or clothes get wet, you'll lose heat more rapidly. Don't dress too heavily. You'll sweat your clothes wet, and in wet weather you want to be sure your outer clothes repel the water. In the rain, your clothes should keep you dry on the outside and dry on the inside too.

In cold weather keep your hands, feet, and head warm and dry. They all lose a lot of heat. Try thin gloves under mittens. The air trapped in between will insulate you, just as two pairs of socks, thin ones under heavy, will do it for your feet. A warm wool or fur hat is the best head covering.

Layer your clothes in cold weather, but wear loose, white clothes in hot.

Chapter Eight

How Electricity in the Air Affects You

"I'm not afraid of thunder," Laura told me. "But still I feel rotten when I'm caught out in a storm. It's a little better indoors, but let me tell you what happened last week. I was bicycling and it began to rumble—those awful thunderclaps. I headed for home, but the rain hit me before I got very far. I had to take shelter in a doorway, and the thunder and lightning were something fierce. A bolt struck not a hundred feet away, I swear."

"Obviously none of it hit you," I said.

"Thank God! But as I stood there my head started to clog up. I also had trouble breathing. I have a touch of asthma, but I was fine only a few minutes before. My joints ached too."

"Are you sure it wasn't just fear?"

"No," she answered thoughtfully. "I knew I was protected in the doorway, but I really felt those symptoms. Storms don't scare me. We have enough of them out here. It was something in the air. You know, I swear I had a 'hot flush' while I was standing there. Oh, I know I'm only thirty, but my mother described them to me when she went through her change. For a minute I thought I was prematurely menopausal."

Laura wasn't at all menopausal, but she was extremely weather sensitive, particularly to positive ions. When a thunderstorm associated with lightning occurs, the air becomes saturated with positive ions, sometimes as many as 1,000 to 2,000 per cubic centimeter. That's a lot of ions, and many people report all sorts of reactions the moment they're exposed.

Laura had only a few of them. Other weather-sensitive people have reported insomnia, irritability, tension, chills, sweats, dizziness and loss of balance, migraines and other types of headaches, visual disturbances, nausea, and vomiting. Some people with heart disease feel much worse. Even healthy weather-sensitive people report heart pain and fluttering during a thunderstorm.

Investigators say that positive ions are bad for you, but they give negative ions a clean bill of health. Interestingly enough, negative ions are plentiful in settings we consider picturesque and peaceful. Mountain valleys with waterfalls have an excess of negative ions, as does the seashore. The unpolluted countryside is rich with them.

When you leave the bucolic behind and come into town, the negative ions grow fewer. We don't find many in the air of city streets, factories, or smog-filled places. Hot, dry desert winds and mountain winds like the infamous foehn bring a steady stream of positive ions with them.

The action of ions on our bodies is complex, but one result occurs in the level of serotonin in our bodies. Positive ions cause serotonin to be released, and negative ions suppress the secretion of the substance. Serotonin is the real villain in the picture, causing all the symptoms that weather-sensitive people dread: irritability, headache, uneasiness, and the rest.

How Ions Make You Feel

Even people who are weather resistant and experience little discomfort when the weather changes feel worse with positive ions and better with negative ones. Earlier I mentioned the terrible winds—the foehn, the mistral, the chinook, and the Santa Ana. Their effects are generally credited to an excess of positive ions.

It's only recently that scientists have begun to ascribe many weather-sensitive reactions to positive ions. But for a long time they have known that ions can affect other life forms. In the plant world, an excess of ions seems to promote growth. Giant cucumbers, barley, oats, lettuce, and peas have been grown in ion-rich air. Oddly, negative and positive ions both seem to produce good results on plants. In the human world, however, only the negative ions help.

Some scientists feel that negative ions clear the pollution out of the air. Others report that ions remove bacteria and viruses, which cuts down the incidence of colds, influenza, and many other diseases.

A great deal of controversy exists about the effects of ions. Some scientists are skeptical about them; others are enthusiastic. The enthusiasts are convinced that positive and negative ions have a tremendous impact on our health as well as on our state of mind.

Dr. Felix Gad Sulman, a researcher from Israel, is a pro-ionist. He has studied the effects of the grim Israeli wind, the sharav. It is so generally accepted as deadly that in Israel its presence can be entered as a mitigating factor in any crime committed when it is blowing.

Dr. Sulman found three ways in which people respond to heavy exposure to positive ions. One is the *serotonin irritation syndrome*, which occurs when an excess of serotonin is produced by the body. The results are headaches, irritability, sleeplessness, heart pain, and the rest of the weather-sensitive syndrome.

A second response to positive ions is the *exhaustion syndrome*. In the exhaustion syndrome, Dr. Sulman says, the body first responds, paradoxically, in a euphoric way because it is stimulated by all those ions to produce adrenaline. Adrenaline causes a burst of energy, but eventually the excessive adrenaline leads to exhaustion. The victim becomes unable to function and the weather-sensitive symptoms then take over.

The third result of positive ions is the *hyperthyroid response*. The thyroid gland is stimulated and produces too much thyroid hormone: Again an instant burst of energy followed by exhaustion, and the familiar round of symptoms from irritation to heart pain sets in.

Overdoses of positive ions, Dr. Sulman believes, are stored in people under thirty, and brief exposures of two or three weeks to winds like the sharav leave young persons invigorated. After that, exhaustion sets in. Older people, who don't store the ions, are exhausted from the start. Dr. Sulman feels this may account for many younger people's enthusiasm when they visit Israel even though they're caught in the sharav.

For another opinion about positive ions, I talked to a German physician who told me about the red smoke of Ettenheim. "It was back in the fifties," he explained. "We had a neurosurgical unit in the hospital there, and for some reason our patient survival rate was excellent. We had fewer cases of thrombosis than anywhere else in Germany.

"We also had a factory that polluted the air with great clouds of red smoke. It colored everything in town, even the women's clothes, and caused continual complaints to the town fathers. Eventually, under pressure and with the new knowledge of environmental pollution—I think your Rachel Carson's *Silent Spring* did it—the factory installed smokestacks. Everyone was happy as the air over Ettenheim cleared up.

"But at the clinic we found, to our shock and surprise, that our postoperative patients began to die at the same rate they did in other clinics. No more remarkably low mortality rate. We never discovered why, but we learned one interesting fact. One of our doctors had been taking measurements of the ions in the air, and he found that when the red smoke was at its worst, there was an unusually high percentage of negative ions all over town.

"Later measurements, after the smoke was cleared up, were normal. I can only conclude that it was the negative ions that helped my patients."

This German physician's conclusions seemed to be borne out not only by Dr. Sulman's work, but by the work of two other somewhat bewildered American researchers. In separate reports a Wisconsin neurosurgeon, Dr. Norman Shealy, and a Florida surgeon, Dr. Edson Andrews, both noted that surgical patients bleed more during the full moon.

On the face of it, this seems ridiculous, even mystical. But there may be a sound reason behind it. When the moon is full, it comes closer to the earth than at other times, and the earth's ionosphere, positively charged on its underside, moves lower. Measurements seem to indicate that when this happens, there are more positive ions around.

It seems a bit improbable, but it is one logical explanation for what sounds like an astrological event, and it not only confirms the report of the two American surgeons, but it also adds some validity to Dr. Sulman's work and the strange case of the red smoke.

Dos and Don'ts

You cannot avoid ions. They are a natural part of the air, but if you experience troubling headaches, irritability, emotional instability, and even sexual problems for no apparent reason, the culprit may be an excess of positive ions.

There are ion counters available and there are machines

that discharge negative ions, but this is still an "iffy" field. Check to see if there is any possible source of positive ions near you. Are you living in a hot, dry, windy area? Are there many thunderstorms in your neighborhood? Is the industrial pollution severe? Industrial pollution can send out both positive and negative ions. Smoking also produces significant amounts of positive ions. So it it is important to ask: Do you live with a heavy smoker?

To see if your symptoms are ion-caused, spend a week in an unpolluted rural setting, which frequently has an excess of negative ions. Whether it takes you away from positive ions or not, it's bound to relax you and help your symptoms disappear.

What Are Sferics and What Do They Do?

Another electrical phenomenon that affects all of us is the long, low-frequency electromagnetic wave. These waves, called *sferics,* are generated by electrical storms and by some artificial sources, and their influence on health is even more disputed than that of ions. Many researchers have been intrigued with them for years.

Sferics first came to the attention of investigators in 1953 at the Munich Traffic Exhibit, where one of the booths had a setup for testing drivers' reaction time. To the surprise of two physicists who were associated with the booth, there were days when people reacted swiftly while on other days the same people's reactions were slow and lethargic.

After discounting all other possible factors, the physicists decided that the only explanation they could offer was an increase in sferics on the days when reaction time was slow.

In the German scientific journal *Naturwissenschaften,* Drs. H. Koenig and F. Ankermuller told how they had subjected a group of people to artificially produced sferics. Within a few moments of the long-wave barrage the volunteers reported a variety of symptoms, ranging from bad headaches to tiredness, difficulty in breathing, and excessive sweating. However, other researchers have been unable to find definite physical reactions like these or to duplicate the experiments.

At the Institut für Balneologie and Klimaphysiologie of the University of Freiburg, I heard a negative reaction to sferics.

I talked to Dr. Werner Ranscht-Froensdorff, a physician at the institute, a "no-nonsense" researcher who had conducted experiments with sferics. "We had six volunteers live for two to four weeks in total isolation in a special electroclimate room, a room shielded against all outside influences and constructed so that we could duplicate any natural climate or electrical system," he told me. "We flooded these people with artificial sferics, changing our program from day to day. At the same time we filled the room with a variety of temperatures and climates."

"And you found?"

He shrugged. "Oh, we found something. We found abnormalities in the blood when we used an enormous amount of sferics, but the abnormalities appeared after we had stopped the sferics, in fact two or three days after."

"What did these abnormalities mean?" I asked.

He shrugged. "They weren't pathological. The effect seemed to be minor. They don't cause any real problems in people. They're simply coagulation changes in the blood."

"But you're talking of healthy people," I protested. "What about the cardiac patient? Couldn't coagulation changes be serious in a man with heart disease? Wouldn't this lead to possible embolisms?"

He nodded, almost reluctantly. "To cardiac patients the changes are significant, but there is no real advice we can give them. What can we say? Stay in a sheltered room? Stay away from electrical machinery that might send out long waves? Leave town during a thunderstorm? No, our findings about sferics are just not significant as far as I'm concerned. We've concluded that they are of no importance in terms of how they affect people."

"But have you any other significant findings about them?"

He looked at me and smiled. "It was significant for us to find out that our findings were not significant."

I had to be content with that. But I'm not sure I agree with Dr. Ranscht-Froensdorff that sferics have no effect on us. Too many other studies indicate that they do. Dr. Reinhold Reiter, director of a physiological biometeorological institute in West Germany, thinks that sferics have a definite effect on humans.

"We asked the Bavarian Bureau of Statistics for the total number of deaths per calendar day in each district of Bavaria to apply sferics to them as an indicator," Dr. Reiter said. "We noted that the frequency of deaths on the days with high sferics is considerably above the norm. It is considerably below the norm on days with low sferics."

On days with strong sferics he found a greater increase in the number of industrial accidents. Since most occurred indoors, he was able to discount the effect of the storm itself and consider only the sferics.

Whatever the facts are about sferics—and there seem to be many that point up their importance as an influence on people—the final results are not yet in. This is an intriguing area of research, one we are just beginning to become aware of in America. Unfortunately, the area of atmospheric electricity is filled with unsavory practitioners as well as qualified researchers. It is a field where a quick buck can be made by trading on people's gullibility, and dozens of machines for promoting healthful ions and sferics are on the market.

Until more solid research is done, we still do not know how important sferics are. All we know is that they do something to our bodies, and that "something" may be good or it may be bad. The bad reports are in; the good ones are still to come. A schoolteacher grading tests that had been taken during a thunderstorm found that his pupils did extraordinarily well. Was it the sferics—or some other still undiscovered psychological factor?

The Fogs of Death

At one point in my European research, I found myself driving through the Meuse Valley from Namur to Liège. At a gas station, while the attendant filled my tank, I talked to the owner, a man in his late seventies, and asked, "Were you here in nineteen thirty?"

He nodded. "Those were terrible times. I lost my father and two cousins."

The young attendant capped my tank and grinned. "What war was that?"

"What do you know of war?" The old man shook his head. "I'll tell you, it was not war. It was the fog! It came in like a live thing rolling up the river. The weather wasn't bad, but that cursed fog lay up and down the valley like a blanket for three days, and it killed so many. The older ones, they began to cough. Their throats would get raw and they couldn't breathe. It was like a band around the chest.

"It was a terrible time. In the war at least there was an enemy to fight. In that terrible fog you could only fight the air."

I drove away troubled by the sadness in that old man's eyes after all these years. I had heard of the Meuse Valley fog. That was why I asked the old man about it. I knew it was a killer. I also knew of a fog in Donora in the United States eighteen years later. In 1948, in a river valley south of Pittsburgh, a large anticyclonic area and a prolonged weather inversion caused a poisonous fog to hang over Donora for three days. Seventeen people died from that fog, mostly older people and many of them cardiac cases.

London had killer fogs in 1952 and 1962. Thousands of people suffered respiratory illness, choking, and coughing. In 1952, 4,000 more people died than could have been expected, according to statistics. In 1962 there were 700 additional deaths.

New York City had its turn in 1953, and again in 1962, the same year that the second London fog occurred.

The cause in each case was man-made pollutants. Sulfur dioxide and smoke were trapped by the fog and held in place by a freak of weather.

As the industrial revolution changed man's life-style, it brought a load of social problems and an overwhelmingly destructive impact on the environment. I never realized this as much as I did after talking to the survivors of the Meuse Valley fog.

I have encountered smog many times. I remember one sunny California day years ago when I visited my brother, who lives on a hill overlooking Los Angeles. Looking out over the city, I asked, "What's all that brown stuff hanging there?"

"Smog," he said, and added reassuringly, "but it never gets up here."

He was right. The pollution didn't get up to him; it did its damage down below. The pollution we pour into our air doesn't always mix and dissipate. Sometimes it hangs motionless in one place, held by a layer of warm air atop a layer of cold air. This so-called temperature inversion traps and holds the smog.

I visited my brother at noon, when the greatest concentration of pollution regularly occurs in Los Angeles. The smog comes from automobile exhausts, and when the sun is strongest, its radiation oxidizes the material in the smog into more deadly gases.

In the valleys of the Alps, where industrialization was stimulated by the availability of water power and then continued with fossil fuels, I have seen clouds of smog hovering over gems of green forests and rivers. That smog, like the London ones, was due to sulfur dioxide, the result of burning coal and fuel oil.

The United States Public Health Service estimated that at least 150 million tons of pollution are emptied into the atmosphere each year. Temperature inversions hold some of this pollution in one place, but eventually it does dissipate. It is often replaced by new smog.

Although it is not strictly part of weather, smog is affected by weather. It is moved by wind and by all the other vagaries of weather.

How pure or how polluted the atmosphere is has a strong influence on the temperature, humidity, and motion of the air, and these factors in turn influence climate and weather.

Slowly, over the years, the atmosphere is becoming more and more unbreathable. Dramatic epidemics of illness and death, like those in the Meuse area, Donora, and London, shock us, but we should also be shocked by those slower deaths that cut down life span. Sooner or later lung cancer, asthma, pneumonia, and emphysema are killers; pollution can start them or aggravate them.

How Nature Pollutes the Air

Most of us respond to warnings about air pollution by shivering dutifully and then changing the subject. After all, the ones most affected are the old, the weak, the sick. *I'm hale and healthy, or if not hale—at least healthy. The weather can shift pollution around all it pleases, but how is that going to affect me?*

The startling thing is that weather pollution has a powerful effect on healthy people as well as sick people, and an even more powerful effect on the weather sensitive.

Pollution of our atmosphere is not something that man has created himself. It has been around for millions of years. It must have been noticed by the first labyrinthodont who flopped out of the water and looked into the atmosphere with startled eyes. The wild sweep of a Devonian forest was probably broken by the cone of an active volcano spewing gas and dust into the air. It's a wonder that the little amphibian at the dawn of time wasn't shocked back into the sea permanently.

In our time, volcanoes such as Krakatoa, Etna, and Vesuvius have poured tons of debris into the atmosphere, and this natural pollution has spread around the globe. It gave us some beautiful sunsets, but also some gritty air to breathe.

These are isolated incidents. On a regular basis, nature pollutes our atmosphere with pollen, spores, and bacteria, with yeast, mold, and mildew. We do react, even those of us who are healthy, to these pollutants of nature. More than 6 percent of us react strongly, with coughing, sneezing, and runny, irritated noses. We call it hay fever, and it is probably as old as man himself.

Some people react very violently to the spores of certain fungi, while others are laid low by mildew or yeast.

In America and in Britain the chief villain is pollen. The ubiquitous nature of pollen was discovered by an English physician, Dr. C. H. Blackley, in the 1870s. He flew sticky kites high in the air, then examined them by microscope and found that they had trapped air-borne pollen.

Of all the pollens that pollute our air, those of ragweed are probably the most virulent. In the United States ragweed grows heavily in the Midwest and parts of the East Coast (Florida and Maine are relatively free of it) and lightly in all the far Western states except Washington.

Wherever pollen is produced, weather spreads it around, and man lends a hand. We seem to insist on aiding anything that can harm us. Originally ragweed grew only in limited areas. The ragweed plant is a tough fighter for survival in the plant world, but it had to struggle for existence with many other plants.

Man, turning up the soil for crops, buildings, and roads, gave the ragweed seeds an edge. He left the ground exposed, and in the botanical free for all that took place, ragweed won out. Now it lines all the Midwestern and Eastern farms, highways, and city lots, sending increasing clouds of invisible pollen into the air.

The pollen is light enough to float, and high winds spread it around. On a windy day during the pollen season, hay-fever sufferers are in agony. Let the weather change, let the rains come—especially long-lasting rains—and the pollen is washed away. They can then breathe a sigh of relief.

The weather starts its work on pollen long before a plant produces it. The amount of rainfall affects the pollen crop, and so does the temperature.

Ragweed is only one of the plants that spreads pollen. Nature is very ingenious in its cunning efforts to let its children reproduce. Dry, warm air will trigger the pollen-release mechanism of one plant; moist air or rain will trigger that of another. Trees raise their flowers high above the ground to give their pollen a better chance for survival. Some, like the pines, release their pollen only in a high wind to ensure that it is spread as far as possible.

Nature has a wasteful way of reproduction in the plant world. It fills the air with millions of microscopic particles of pollen, all on the chance that one or two will strike each flower and start a seed. It gives us a frightening picture of a season when the atmosphere is choked and polluted with pollen. Is there no escape?

Dos and Don'ts

If you have any respiratory illness, heart disease, asthmatic condition, or if you are over sixty, pollution alerts should be of vital concern to you. If you hear on the weather report that the air quality is unsatisfactory, try your damnedest to get out of town. If you can't manage that, stay indoors and limit your activity. Don't overexert yourself.

If you are weather sensitive and react to smog, now is the time to take it easy. It's best not to drive, not only because the smog can impair your judgment, but because you'll be adding more pollution to the air.

Everyone, weather sensitive or not, is damaged to some degree by smog. We should be aware when pollution is held suspended by a temperature inversion. It's a time to limit your activity and the stress you may be undergoing. Don't take on any unrealistic deadlines. Don't get into serious arguments.

If you live in an area with a smog problem, it may be time to contact your environmental protection agency and see what you can do as a private citizen to help fight it.

There are vast areas in the United States that are almost pollen-free, or at least haven't enough pollen to affect us. I mentioned before that ragweed is limited to the Midwest and parts of the East Coast. California is nearly pollen clear, as are Oregon, Nevada, Idaho, and Colorado.

Plants act as natural filters for pollen. Their leaves become loaded with it in the areas where it is produced. If you are troubled by allergies, stay away from those beautiful forests and woodlands or, if you must be there, pick a coastal area where the wind comes in from the sea and blows the pollen inland. An island is usually pollen-free because winds sweep over it and keep its air clean.

Rain washes the air free of pollen, and weather sensitives can wander through the woods after a rainstorm with some safety. Air conditioning doesn't do much for pollen sufferers unless there are filters in the system fine enough to pick up the pollen grains. I have a friend with a lovely summer house in a cool, woody hollow, and on the hottest day his house is comfortable. Still he has an air conditioner. When I asked him why, he shrugged. "Not for cooling, but for filtering the air. I have an electronic cleaning system that delivers pollen-free air all through the house, and it's worth it—no dust, no sneezes."

Chapter Nine

How the Weather Affects Your Mind

Charles is an attendant at one of the psychiatric institutes in Topeka. "It's a good job," he told me. "I like helping people —but the thing is, I can't take the weather. It is so extreme— hot one day and cold a few hours later."

"Does it affect the patients?" I asked.

He shook his head. "Man, does it ever! I can tell when the weather is getting warmer by the way they act. Never mind what I feel, or what the thermometer says; when there's a sudden change from cold to warm, they start acting up, shouting and picking fights with each other, and just like clockwork they turn off when the weather gets cold again. It's the weirdest thing."

Weird to Charles, perhaps, but not uncommon. Dr. Tromp had heard of this reaction and he started a study with twenty-one psychiatrists at seven psychiatric institutes in Europe to investigate the effects of weather on mental patients.

A daily log of patient restlessness was kept and matched against weather conditions. His findings confirmed what attendants like Charles know empirically; warm air masses moving into an area upset psychiatric patients and make them restless and uneasy.

When the warm air mass is accompanied by strong winds or by rain, the patients became even more upset. Some get out of hand altogether.

Dr. Tromp also found that cold air masses had the opposite effect: The patients became quieter than usual.

A careful check of all other weather elements showed that none was significant in this case. Barometric pressure, wind, humidity, lightning storms—none of them had the same effect as the advent of masses of warm or cold air. This is a very restricted kind of weather sensitivity.

If a change in the weather could influence the way emotionally disturbed people acted, could such a change have anything to do, even indirectly, with people *becoming* emotionally disturbed? Does weather help to cause mental illness?

A California psychiatrist I spoke to pointed out that for years men had linked the moon to insanity. "That's how we got the word 'lunatic,' from lunar. I suppose the phases of the moon could be considered weather."

"But you don't really believe in the moon's effect?"

"To mangle Shakespeare, our madness lies not in our stars, but in our parents. Now let's talk about family environment. . . ."

Another psychiatrist was inclined to take the lunar effect more seriously. "You know, of course," he told me, "that more children are delivered when there's a full moon. There was a study done some time ago that proved it. There is no doubt that the weather affects our body—you've found that out by now. Why should there be any doubt that it affects our minds?

"I would suggest you get in touch with Dr. Volker Faust. I've read some of his articles and he's a competent researcher."

Meeting Dr. Faust

I had heard of Dr. Faust, and I did go to see him. (Earlier in the book I quoted some of what he told me about adaptation.) Dr. Faust is a psychiatrist and I met him one rainy night in a psychiatric institute near the small German town of Bad Krozingen, a few miles from the French border.

Dark-haired, young, intense, and a bit didactic, Dr. Faust has spent many years studying the impact of weather on the mind. "I used to work at a clinic in Basel, Switzerland, an area of many barometric changes," he told me. "We had an unusually large number of emotionally disturbed patients, and I always wondered if there was a connection with the weather. What convinced me was a study I did, a comparison between one thousand mentally disturbed patients and one thousand healthy people. I was left with no doubt. The weather affected everyone, but many more of the disturbed patients became upset.

"I asked myself: The mental patients who come to the clinic are sick, and have been sick for a while—why did they pick this particular day to sign in? The reason might well be the weather.

"I checked it out by comparing hospital admissions with the weather over a period of two to three years. I studied the records of seventeen thousand, three hundred and eighty patients and found a very definite correlation. The bad weather comes and our number of admissions goes up. I would say, offhand, that fifty percent of mental patients are extremely weather sensitive.

"Weather sensitivity," he went on, "is not an illness. It is an indicator of one's health. We are all weather sensitive to some degree. When we are disturbed, our sensitivity increases."

"Do you agree with the researchers who found a thirty percent weather sensitivity in the general population?" I asked.

He shrugged. "Yes. But it's a range, remember. Only twenty percent of children are extremely weather sensitive, whereas fifty percent of older people are. You know, I have studied weather sensitivity in terms of social classes."

"What did you find?"

"The lowest economic class in society and the highest are the most sensitive. The middle class is the least—but—" He grinned. "It has nothing to do with class."

Bewildered, I said, "You just told me . . ."

"I'm confusing you deliberately. You see, it's how you use your body. The people in the lowest class, the working class, are weather sensitive because they have weather-sensitive bodies. Their backs, their joints—hard work has damaged them. The upper class and the intellectuals react differently— not with their bodies but with their minds. They have trouble sleeping, concentrating."

"And when an intellectual is physically active, as many are back home—what with jogging and tennis?"

"Poor man, he feels it all over!"

"Have you found any difference in the way your various types of mental patients react to weather?" I asked.

"Oh yes. Schizophrenics are most susceptible to warm, dry winds and both warm and cold fronts. Neurotics react strongly to cold fronts. Depressives are susceptible to warm and cold fronts as well as occlusions and warm, dry winds.

"It's a funny thing. Schizophrenics, who are so weather sensitive, don't appear to be when you question them. The same is true for alcoholics for different, yet similar, reasons."

"What are the reasons?"

"Schizophrenics are so out of touch with reality, they don't recognize their own sensitivity. Alcoholics are so poisoned by drink that their brains are damaged, and they too can't recognize their own sensitivity. Objectively, both are affected."

"Have your studies shown that the weather affects suicides?"

"There are more suicides in bad weather, yes. It's the

weather that may give that final push, but the man or woman must be ready to kill himself or herself. There are many suicides on bright, sunny days. It's as if the suicide can't bear to be so unhappy when everyone else is happy. Even the day and weather seem in league to point out his miserable state.

"You talk of the weather affecting people, and it does, but to turn it around, weather-sensitive people are psychologically volatile, moody, ready to go up or down. It's not just the weather. It's their own emotional nature."

Times You Should Watch

I thought about what Dr. Faust told me that night and wondered: If weather is so important a factor in precipitating crises in troubled people, what about those of us who are not troubled, or at least no more troubled than the average person? Can an abrupt change in the weather affect behavior?

Of the many people I interviewed—not scientists, but ordinary men and women—many said they were affected emotionally by changes in the weather. Rosa and Allen are a young couple living together before they get married. "I don't think we'll make a go of it," Rosa told me. "I suppose it's my fault. For no reason at all, I'll get moody, depressed—we broke up three weeks ago, the night of that big thunderstorm. I blew up at nothing and raged out of the apartment with my suitcase. I went home to mom—a crazy thing. Then Allen and I met in the street two days later and fell into each other's arms. We're living together again, but I don't know. We've done this before."

It wasn't hard to link Rosa's emotional outburst to the thunderstorms. When she became aware of it, she was amazed that she never had noticed it. "It's so regular—a storm blows in and I blow up, like clockwork!"

Marjorie, a student at Kirkland College near Utica, in New York's snow belt, told me, "We go stir crazy during those long winter months. That white snow everywhere, and spring never seems to come. We begin to fight with each other in March and April. In the dorms we're at each other's throats and that's when the dropouts start. You just can't take it!"

Eva, a Swedish girl, told me, "Back home the long, dark winter is dreadful. When spring comes, our minds turn over. We are all filled with a kind of euphoria. It's spring madness!" Over here we call it spring fever.

Jim, who heads a construction crew in western Connecticut, told me thoughtfully, "I haven't stopped to figure out just what it is, but when there's a certain kind of bad weather I watch out. Last week it turned cold suddenly, and one of my best workers, a really careful guy, almost took his arm off with a portable saw. I don't know if it was the cold or the sudden change, but I've seen it happen again and again."

Rosa, Marjorie, and Eva were emotionally affected by the weather. I have no doubt of that, just as I have no doubt that a cold front over Connecticut caused the accident to Jim's worker.

Proof that fronts can influence people to become careless and accident-prone comes from Poland. There, two Polish scientists demonstrated scientifically what Jim knew from experience. They correlated almost two thousand accidents among construction workers between 1966 and 1970 throughout Poland with the weather for each day an accident occurred in terms of fronts, barometric pressure, and winds.

They found that the weather did affect the average mentally stable worker. The passage of cold fronts increased the number of accidents; in fact, work accidents were twice as frequent during cyclonic situations as they were during anticyclonic situations. Nor was the physical effect responsible— the impact of the wind on the construction and the workers. During cyclonic times, testing also showed a decrease in mental and physical efficiency.

They further found, when they studied yearly records, that there were many more accidents in the fall and spring, the seasons of particularly variable weather in Poland.

Dr. Harflinger, the Freiburg biometeorologist, found in his massive study of the workers at the Mercedes-Benz auto plant in Stuttgart that there, too, accidents were directly related to the weather.

If the weather has so great an effect on psychiatric patients and on normal construction and factory workers, what about the rest of us? How weather sensitive are we in terms of mental outlook? Can an abrupt change in the weather—or any change of climate—affect emotional stability, concentration, judgment, and discrimination?

In May 1977, an article in the *New York Times* reported that traffic deaths rose as the weather changed for the better. After a 10 percent decrease in January and a 4 percent drop in February, when winter was severe, March accidents rose by 8 percent.

One's immediate reaction is, "Of course. More people travel once the weather improves. There would, therefore, be more accidents." But the studies took the increase in travelers into account. And this link between traffic accidents and the weather is not confined to the United States. It exists all over the world, and a Polish researcher began to wonder why the increase in the percentage of accidents was higher than the increase in the percentage of people on the road in bitter weather.

Statistically compensating for the increase in the number of drivers, he gave psychological tests to accident victims to determine their weather sensitivity. He found that at least half the people involved in "difficult traffic situations" were sensitive to weather. He also discovered that there had been weather disturbances—low barometers, warm and cold fronts, disturbed highs, or occlusions—during more than 90 percent of the traffic accidents!

There is no reason to stop driving on weather-active days, but it's a good reason to be more cautious.

No two of us react to weather in the same way. Some of us—typical snow babies—love the cold. When the thermometer drops we breathe a sigh of relief and head for our skis and the slopes. Others are attuned to heat. They beg, borrow, and steal to fly south when winter comes. Some of us hate the rain and others glory in it, treating raincoats and umbrellas with disdain.

I know one young man in his thirties who lives in mountainous upstate New York. Dan heats his cabin with firewood and thinks nothing of going out on the coldest days in jeans and a T-shirt to bring in a load of wood. His friend John, who shared the cabin with him one winter, said, "He's mad! All I'd have to do is step out into that cold without my arctic jacket and I'd freeze my ass off. I'd be a lump of ice!"

What makes one person capable of enduring abrupt changes in weather while another is sensitive to the slightest variation? Are there clues in our personalities? To find out, two German scientists talked eighteen healthy young men into a brave experiment. For a space of two weeks they had these volunteers expose themselves to temperatures as low as 40° Fahrenheit.

A mass of physiological data was recorded without revealing much, but psychological testing produced one fascinating fact: Those able to take the cold in their stride were less nervous and inhibited than the others and had more self-confidence, more of the quality the male German researchers in their possibly sexist wisdom labeled *masculinity*.

Intrigued, I thought of my friend Dan and his cabin mate for that winter, John. There was no doubt that they fit the research model. Dan is outgoing, stable, and indeed, a very *masculine* man. John is more sensitive, inhibited, and not at all self-confident!

Dos and Don'ts

Determine your own weather sensitivity in terms of your emotions. Are you moody or depressed during stormy weather, or does rough weather elate you?

Keep a chart of how you feel each day—mood swings, headaches, etc.—and what the weather pattern is. A month is enough to give you a representative sample. Do your moods change before fronts pass over, during the weather upset accompanying the passage of the front, or during the warm or cold weather that follows? Check against temperatures, humidity, and barometric pressure.

Once you have determined the connection, plan ahead. If you must do dangerous work or drive a car on those days, be extra-cautious. Alert your coworkers, wife, husband, or lover, so they can take your moods more in stride. Remember: Mood changes can be managed if you are aware of what causes them, and headaches will usually yield to aspirin. Awareness is the essential key to coping.

If you are the parent of a normal, healthy child who suddenly becomes moody for no apparent reason, study the weather map. Does your child become irritable or overactive when the barometer is high or when the weather changes from cold to warm? Remember, one out of every five children is weather sensitive—but most are too young to tell you just what bothers them.

If you work at any outdoor job, be especially careful on days when a cold front moves in. Remember, accidents happen to competent people who are weather sensitive, and they are more likely to happen on turbulent days.

Chapter Ten

How the Stars Affect Your Weather Sensitivity

Doris is in her early thirties, attractive but with a lingering unhappiness in her face. I talked to her in a playground near her home. "I can't help thinking that the long, hot summer had something to do with it," Doris told me quietly as we watched her eight-year-old playing in the sandbox. Alan was retarded—physically a beautiful little boy but mentally forever a four-year-old.

I tried, without success, to think of something comforting to say, but Doris was caught up in her own memories. "Alan was conceived in April," she murmured, "and we were very happy about it. We really wanted a child, and we had been trying for so long. The pregnancy was easy at first, but that July was unbearably hot, and I was so miserable—I don't know. It just seems as if something happened then. I can't tell what, but I'm sure the heat had something to do with Alan's brain damage."

Doris's conviction that the terribly hot summer was in some way responsible for Alan's problem may be based on more than intuition. There is scientific evidence that the month of a child's birth can be related to mental problems of various kinds. This is not an astrological fantasy, but a conclusion based on the work of a respected husband-and-wife research team.

Dr. Benjamin Pasamanick was director of the Research Division of the Columbus Psychiatric Institute in Ohio when he and his wife, Dr. Hilda Knobloch, a noted pediatrician, worked together on a study that at first seemed to be nothing but astrology. They found that more schizophrenics were born in January, February, and March—and therefore conceived in April, May, and June. The third month after conception, the researchers pointed out, is when the cerebral cortex of the child develops: for these children, June, July, and August.

The doctors concluded that the only factor that could influence these children's mental development was the weather. They reasoned that high temperatures and a decreased protein intake (two things likely to happen in hot summers) could affect the developing fetal brain.

Further study of birth dates and mental problems showed still another clear-cut relationship. There were more mentally damaged children born after hot summers than after cool ones. The doctors were also able to demonstrate that more children with all types of birth defects were born in January, February, and March than at any other time of the year. Again, the hot summer was held responsible.

Confirmation of their results came from another study, this one of 15,000 schizophrenics in Great Britain and the Netherlands. Again the relationship between the summer and mental damage held true. More schizophrenic children were born after a severely hot summer. In Moscow, instead of studying children with schizophrenia or mental retardation, researchers matched IQ scores of schoolchildren with their dates of birth and found a similar link. Since IQ's are strongly affected by cultural influences, this is hardly conclusive; it does furnish some additional confirmation.

All evidence seems to indicate that either a dietary deficiency brought on by the heat, or the heat itself, produces inadequate development and mental problems. Of course not every child born after a hot summer will suffer, but a statistically significant number will be abnormal.

The connection is close enough, some researchers suggest, to warn would-be parents to arrange conception so that the child will be born between July and December. This is particularly true if there is any history of mental problems in the family. The researchers suspect that a genetic tendency might be exaggerated by excessive hot weather during that crucial three-month period of pregnancy.

Seeing Light with Your Third Eye

The developing brain of a human embryo is particularly sensitive to extreme heat, but what causes a fully developed human brain to be affected by changes in the weather? Is there a physiological reason why the sudden advent of warm air masses can upset mental patients?

A careful examination of the blood chemistry of schizophrenics turned up a clue. A Canadian researcher found that their blood contains a potentially poisonous substance. He couldn't isolate the substance, but in laboratory tests he found that serum from the blood of schizophrenics, drawn on ordinary days, killed tadpoles when it was added to the water in their tank. If the blood was taken when there was a drastic weather change, the serum was harmless. The toxic substance in the blood seemed to disappear when the weather changed. It seems reasonable to infer that if this blood toxin is related to mental disease, and disappears when the weather changes, then there must be a link between weather and mental health, the exact nature of which is still unknown.

Further research into the behavior of mental patients during sudden temperature changes revealed that during the early winter months—November, December, and January—there is more unrest than at any other time. This is not the coldest part of the winter, but it is the darkest, the time of failing light. The days grow shorter and shorter until on December 22, we reach the winter solstice, the longest night of the year.

In antiquity people were aware of the peculiar significance of the night of the winter solstice. They dreaded the shortening days, and feared that unless something was done to check the failing light, the days would keep growing shorter until eventually there would be no light, no sun at all!

On the night of the winter solstice, they built huge bonfires to encourage the sun and fend off the encroaching dark. They decorated sacred trees, created elaborate ceremonies and rituals around the solstice, sacrificed their finest animals and even an occasional virgin, "lest darkness fall."

Old wives' tales? Perhaps. Yet this dread of the dark seems to be one of man's few eternal instincts. The dark is a time of ghosts and witches, of fear and uneasiness. Perhaps the dread is a genetic inheritance from those primitive times when the most deadly predators were the nocturnal ones. People who feared the dark were better able to survive; and over the course of evolution an aversion to darkness and a love of light has been bred into man.

When we see the days growing shorter we become uneasy. Intellectually we know they'll lengthen again as the earth completes its swing around the sun, but on an emotional level that fear persists. Light, not cold, becomes the principal weather factor affecting our emotional stability.

We don't have to be mentally disturbed to feel the influence of the shorter days. We are all familiar with the general gloom that hits us when the sun is hidden by clouds. Given three or four days of rain and sunless skies, a gradual depression settles on everyone.

Another reason we are so tied to light may lie in the structure of the brain. One part of the brain is light sensitive; it is probably the part that was once, in primitive reptiles, a third eye. In humans it has become the pineal gland. Sensing its importance, but not knowing what it did, some early philosophers speculated that it might be the seat of the soul. A more scientific interpretation was suggested by Dr. Richard J. Wurtman of Boston's Massachusetts General Hospital. In experiments with blind girls, Dr. Wurtman found that girls who were blind from birth menstruated early in life; girls born albino and receiving too much light through their pigmentless eyes started their menstrual periods later than most girls.

What causes this, according to Dr. Wurtman, may well be the mysterious pineal gland. "It is possible," he speculated, "that one role of this gland is to serve as a neuroendocrine transducer [a hormone that influences the nervous system] for converting information about environmental light into a hormonal message.

"Light," he explained, "by way of the pineal gland and other brain centers, sets the stage for puberty and the onset of menstruation." Further experiments with boys confirmed the fact that light also affects the development of male puberty.

Dr. Wurtman's experiments explain mankind's enduring love of sunlight. The dependence of puberty on light is probably only one of our many hormonal relationships to the sun.

Sudden cold can affect mental health and so can winter's failing light. Another indirect influence of the weather on our mental health can come when the weather wakes us up at the wrong time.

One of my uncles used to arrive at breakfast each morning with one of two comments. It was either a satisfied "I slept like a log last night. Not a dream!" or a grumpy "I dreamed all night!" He saw dreaming as an intrusion on his sleep, something he couldn't control and thoroughly detested.

Neither of his statements was right. I doubt if anyone spends a night without dreaming, any more than he spends the entire night dreaming. Researchers from New York's Mount Sinai Hospital, where a large number of sleep studies have been carried out, proved that we all dream and we dream in intervals. During a night's sleep, there are periods of dreaming, followed by periods of dreamless sleep. Observers can tell when a sleeper dreams by the rapid movements of his or her eyes behind closed lids. This dreaming sleep is called rapid eye movement (REM) sleep.

If we are awakened between dreaming periods, wakened out of that sound and dreamless sleep my uncle craved, then it makes no difference to our health. But if we are awakened from a dreaming period, it's another matter. Then, according to the Mount Sinai researchers, we can experience psychological upsets during the following day.

America is a nation of open-window sleepers, and because of this we are particularly vulnerable to weather changes at night. We may fall asleep at a comfortable temperature, covered with a light blanket. During the night a sudden change in weather can cause the temperature to fall. The center in the brain that regulates body heat is disturbed and communicates with the sleep center: "Get this body up and into something warm!"

We wake up at once, shivering, often from a dreaming period. When this happens, we cannot understand our emotional disturbance the next day. By then the weather outside may be perfect, and we get no obvious weather-related clues.

The same effect takes place with a rise in temperature and an excess of heat under the blankets. House thermostats are either off or down for the night, and unless we are sleeping in a temperature-controlled, air-conditioned room, we are at the mercy of the outside weather.

The Earthquake Factor

Astrology, so long fallen into disrepute, has recently had a popular resurgence, so much so that some otherwise sober scientists are taking a second look at it. The work of Drs. Pasamanick and Knobloch seems to link science and astrology. So does the work of Michel Guaquelin.

Dr. Faust, the sensible psychiatrist I talked to in Germany, suggested seriously that I talk to M. Guaquelin. "He has some unusual theories about the planets and their influence on weather and on people."

Guaquelin has done his research at the Psychophysiological Laboratory at Strasbourg in France. His theory is that long electromagnetic waves (sferics), coming from outer space, sometimes penetrate our atmosphere and affect us. The sun is a source of some of these sferics, but Guaquelin believes that the moon sometimes blocks the sferics, and so do Venus, Mars, and Jupiter.

He postulates a complex electromagnetic interaction between the sun, the planets, and even the distant stars. He has uncovered unusual statistics to bolster his theory, including a survey of 100,000 births showing that "infants are born under the same planetary conditions that prevailed at the birth of their parents."

He cites many studies suggesting how the moon influences us: an increase in crime during the full moon, a connection between deaths, pneumonia, blood disorders, and even the sex of children and the phases of the moon.

He links increased sunspot activity to the terrible plagues of history, typhus and cholera, smallpox and diphtheria, and his research seems sound. Whether this is fact is still not certain. Other studies do seem to confirm at least the sunspot influence that Guaquelin writes about.

A report in the *New York Times* about the most powerful

recorded eruption on the sun said: "The most immediate effect of yesterday's flare-up was a flash of X rays . . . One of the most dramatic effects . . . was the manner in which magnetic fields, blasted into space with material ejected from the flare, cut off cosmic rays from beyond the solar system."

To attempt to assess solar impact, a Canadian psychiatrist, Dr. Heinz Lehman, matched hostile outbreaks in psychiatric patients at Canada's Douglas Hospital against many factors and found a surprising correlation with solar flares and sunspots.

"Such flares," he explained, "flood the earth with high-energy particles and influence magnetic fields. It has long been known that people who work close to high-density, pulsed electromagnetic energy, like that found in lightning bolts, are disturbed in their thinking."

The effect of electric waves has already been discussed, but magnetic fields too have a powerful impact on our lives. People have been aware of these effects for thousands of years. Mary Renault, in one of her books about legendary Greece, wrote of Theseus and his ability to anticipate earthquakes. In the novel, his ability comes from his father, the god Poseidon, who conferred the gift on him. But this ability may not be only a pleasant novelistic invention. Many such stories of earthquake-sensitive people are known, and today in China some research has been done on the abilities of various animals to detect incipient quakes.

A friend of mine told me that he discovered this earthquake sensitivity in himself while working with an archaeological expedition in Costa Rica. "I was in the dig under a very tall cliff when I suddenly felt an overwhelming urge to get out in the open. It was almost a sense of nausea. I climbed out of the pit and hurried to the center of an open field nearby. It was a sunlit, beautiful day, and I couldn't understand what was troubling me.

"Then all at once I felt the ground heave under my feet. I

was thrown down, and I scrambled up and kept my balance with difficulty. Afterwards I stood there shaking as much as the earth had. Later, I found out that the walls of the dig had collapsed. I don't know what sense drove me out, but thank God for it!"

Another friend from Los Angeles told me of her prescience about a recent severe quake in that city. "I woke up the night before the quake and shook my husband. When he sat up, bewildered, I said, 'Jack, I'm getting out of town tonight.' He said, 'Moira, you're crazy—get back to sleep. It's three o'clock in the morning!' I couldn't get him up, and to tell the truth I didn't know myself what bothered me. I just felt apprehensive—sick with apprehension—and I wanted to get out and run."

The next night, she said, at exactly 3:00 A.M., the quake struck the city. They weren't hurt, but they were shaken up.

The exact twenty-four-hour warning may be coincidence or a stretching of the facts, but her husband assured me she did wake up and try to get him to leave. Her anxiety and my archaeologist friend's "sense" that drove him out in the open may both have been reactions to the high-intensity electric fields that appear before earthquakes.

Some areas that are prone to earthquakes produce smaller electric fields for weeks before any quake takes place. Depending on the strength of these fields, all sorts of strange and puzzling things can happen to people who are nearby.

The hippocampus is, electrically, the most unstable part of the brain. When it is stimulated by a strong electric field, reactions range from nausea to visions and hallucinations. Lesser fields cause difficulties in sleeping, strange sensations, feelings of apprehensiveness, and disturbances in hearing and balance.

In other words, there are indeed sensitive people like my friends who can anticipate the coming of quakes. In ancient times this was accepted as a warning from the gods. In

Renault's book, Theseus believed that Poseidon sent the warnings. If there ever was a Theseus, he probably had a particularly sensitive hippocampus.

Today we are coming to understand the effects of electrical and magnetic fields. For many years such fields were ignored or considered the province of cranks. At the turn of the century electrical devices were sold for every ailment from cancer to bedwetting. The devices were bulky sets of batteries built into clothes and they were supposed to bathe the wearer with healing electrical waves.

As people began to understand more about electricity, they realized how fraudulent these claims were, and the idea that electric fields could affect the body in such ways fell into disrepute.

Recent years have seen a revival of interest in the effects of magnetic and electric fields. The realization that some people are earthquake sensitive is one result of that interest.

How the Earth's Magnetic Fields Affect You

Of the many experiments with animals placed in magnetic and electric fields, a rather unusual one showed that when rats were exposed to magnetic fields during pregnancy, their offspring were more "emotional" than the offspring of rats who weren't exposed. Does the same thing hold true for humans?

Since the magnetic activity of the earth has been charted for many years, it was possible for a team of Canadian researchers to study adults who had been exposed to increased magnetic activity for a week before and after they were born. They were given personality tests to see if they were any more anxious than others who had not been born under the same magnetic conditions.

The researchers found that increased magnetic activity of the earth, at birth, did cause long-term anxiety in many people. How this happens is still a mystery, but so is much of the influence of weather on humans. Much that we put down as superstition, charlatanism, or astrological mysticism may, after further investigation, turn out to have a scientific basis.

Many years ago one of my brothers told me with some excitement that a local man, a dowser or water finder, had discovered water on his land by using a forked hickory stick. "He gave me the stick," my brother said, "and I walked the area he told me to, holding the stick extended, and sure enough, the stick trembled in my hands at the same spot. We drilled there and found water. The dowser told me I had the power!"

I laughed at the idea of the "power" then, but Yves Rocard, professor of physics at the Sorbonne, holds that our sensitivity to magnetic fields is such that when we stretch our arms taut and balance a long stick (as a dowser does), our nerves and muscles are tense enough to become sensitive to small changes in magnetic field strength.

Professor Rocard tested his theory by placing artificial electric fields underground. He powered them with electric current and found that even weak ones affected the tense muscles and outstretched stick. When we add to this the fact that underground water can create magnetic fields, the dowser's "power" is not so strange after all.

Dos and Don'ts

If you plan to have a baby, try to arrange for it to be born between July and December. While the evidence that conception in April or May increases the chance of a birth defect is still sketchy, enough data exist to warrant caution. If your child is unplanned and you are in your third month of pregnancy in July or August, try to spend it in a cool place. If you have to be in a hot climate during those months, be sure you get all the protein you need.

If you sleep with your windows open and cannot understand your moodiness the next day, try to match it against periods of wakefulness and dreaming. Keep a pad by the bed and if you wake up shivering or sweating jot down whether you were dreaming or not. If you can make the connection, try closing your windows and setting the thermostat for a comfortable temperature. We know now that while the night air is not bad for us, it's not particularly good either. The value of fresh air is an outdated myth. The air outside may be more polluted than that inside.

As for sunspot activity, there's nothing we can do about that. Nineteen seventy-eight brought the most powerful solar eruption ever recorded, but we may be nearing the peak of an eleven-year sunspot cycle. We can't shield ourselves from sunspot activity and the magnetic clouds the sun sends out, but we can expect things soon to return to normal.

During those long, dreary winter days when the sun never seems to shine, take heart. Maybe those temper flare-ups, those moments of depression, those outbursts of unexpected tears are nothing but old buried fears of the sun deserting our planet. Remember, if winter comes, spring cannot be far behind.

As for the winter solstice, lighting bonfires on tall hills as did the pagans won't cause the days to grow longer. Still, a mini-version—lighting candles that night—might be fun.

Chapter Eleven

How Weather Affects Your Heart

Max said, "You know, I run a high blood pressure. I've got arteriosclerosis—you know, when the blood vessels get hard and can't expand. My heart has to work like hell to pump the blood through my body."

I nodded. Max and I were having "coffee *and.*" "And," for Max, was three doughnuts. He ate them apologetically, wedged uncomfortably into the coffee-shop booth. "I have to take off weight. That's what the doctor's been telling me. He said my cholesterol was sky high, and he put me on a diet."

"And you can't stick with it?"

"I'm too anxious. I went back to his office fatter than ever, but you know, my cholesterol was down."

"No kidding! What did he say to that?"

"That's what I think is so crazy. He said it must be the weather."

"What kind of a day was it?"

"Well, not that bad. It was warm when I went in and cold

when I came out. It was raining for a while too, kind of mixed-up weather."

From Max's description, I assumed it was an occluded front, that rainy condition when a warm air mass is overtaken by a cold one, but it didn't seem possible that this was the weather the doctor meant. Had Max been away during that month?

He shrugged. No, he hadn't traveled and the weather was—well, ordinary for April.

I spoke to Max's cardiologist later, and he shook his head. "I give up on him. To break all my rules and come in with a lower cholesterol!"

"You told him it might be the weather."

"I thought it was a possibility. I came across some interesting facts in a medical journal. A Hungarian doctor found that when there were cold fronts near the ground or an occluded front, cholesterol levels dropped by ten percent."

"That was the day Max visited you."

"It was. I went out of my way to check it." He shook his head. "I also discovered that when subtropical air masses move in, the cholesterol level drops twenty percent. I'm seriously thinking of shipping Max off to some place that gets that kind of weather—maybe a southern state near the Gulf."

I laughed. "Max? You'll never get him that far from Broadway!"

Another curious fact that the cardiologist pointed out was that cholesterol levels increase the day before a magnetic storm. The day of the storm, they drop to a shade above normal, and afterwards they fall below normal.

What does it all mean? He shook his head. The researchers didn't know why it happened, but it might eventually lead to climate therapy.

Can Climate Therapy Help You?

That phrase, "climate therapy," interested me. I know that tuberculosis was once treated by sending sufferers up to high altitudes, but for years climate therapy has been out of favor. Was it coming back now?

To find an answer, I spoke to Dr. Helmut E. Landsberg, research professor and chairman of the Graduate Committee on Meteorology at the University of Maryland. Dr. Landsberg was Director of Climatology at the United States Weather Bureau.

"People with heart and circulatory disturbances should avoid very cold weather and very hot weather," he told me. "The stress of either can hurt them, even precipitate heart attacks. If they're thinking of resettling, they should look for a climate that is mild and stable. They have difficulties coping with rapid weather changes."

"So you think they should change their climate?"

"That's a stress too. Still, cold is bad for them. Heart attacks peak in January and February."

"But isn't that because of snow shoveling? It seems that every winter I hear story after story about men who keel over shoveling their walks."

He shook his head. "That may be true here in North America and, I suppose, in Northern Europe. The exertion of snow shoveling is quite a strain and it can cause a heart attack. But it's not true for the rest of Europe. Older people there work just as hard gardening in the spring and summer, and still the greatest number of heart attacks occur in the coldest months.

"No. There's a definite effect of chilling in the winter which causes stress to the heart. If you have angina and you walk against a cold wind, you get chest pains. It's the lack of coronary circulation when you're under weather stress.

"Dr. S. L. Andelman, a former Chicago health commissioner, has an interesting theory about all this. He feels that exertion in the cold isn't the immediate cause of heart attacks, even when you shovel snow. According to him, breathing in a lot of cold air chills your cardiopulmonary system—your heart, lungs, and blood vessels—and that's what brings on the attack."

I thought of what Dr. Landsberg told me when I studied Dr. Tromp's work on cold stress. The Dutch biometeorologist has delved deeply into the stress of cold on the heart. He agrees that the highest mortality from arteriosclerotic heart disease occurs during the coldest months of the year. But he also feels that cold stress, the impact of cold on the entire body, causes blood pressure to rise and at the same time makes us secrete an excess of adrenaline, which causes blood to clot more quickly. This combination of higher blood pressure and quicker clotting is not good for us. The blood, under pressure, can force a clot loose and send it through the body. If it lands in an artery that feeds the heart and blocks off that artery, a part of the heart will become oxygen starved. The result is *myocardial infarction*—damage to the heart muscle and a heart attack.

At the University of Frankfurt in Germany, Drs. H. F. Flodung and F. Becker studied a hundred cases of sudden heart failure and found that many occurred when cold fronts passed over. Nearer to home, the Bureau of the Census in Washington showed a significant relationship between the cold of autumn and winter and angina pectoris and coronary heart disease. In England, scientists found the greatest amount of arteriosclerotic heart disease occurred during January and February, the least during July and August.

In Texas, however, the reverse was true. There, very hot summers brought on more heart attacks than the mild winters. In very hot climates the body works hard to keep its temperature normal by increasing the flow of blood in the skin, hands, and feet. The blood from the deeper parts of the body tries to lose its heat this way by flowing nearer the skin. But this places a strain on the body's circulation and, of course, on the heart.

Dr. Joseph Gold, professor of pharmacology at Upstate Medical Center in Syracuse, New York, says that heart rate reflects heat stress. Heat affects the heart more than anything else in the cardiovascular system. It speeds up the beat, and the more we can tolerate this rapid rate the better we can take the stress. Those of us who are in poor condition, obese, or with heart trouble can't survive this revved-up beat.

Although the stress of hot or cold weather can cause heart attacks, not all these attacks come when we're out shoveling snow or working in the heat. Most of them occur while we are indoors, sleeping or resting. If this is true, then is weather a major factor? Dr. Tromp believes it is.

It boils down to this: Weather such as extreme cold or heat can trigger heart attacks. One factor running through many studies suggests that heart attacks and strokes often come a few days *after* the weather changes. Would this allow time enough to do something about the attacks?

I talked to a member of the volunteer fire department of a small town in the Mildwest. "What we'd like in our department," he told me, "is some way of forecasting heart-attack weather a few days in advance. That would be terrific."

"Why?" I asked.

"Then we could have all our fire and rescue ambulance apparatus ready and we could be sure our stations were manned. Most of us are volunteers here, but if we knew that a particular weekend was going to be troublesome, we'd be on hand. As it is, the only weather we're really sure about is heat. We know we get a twenty percent increase in heart attacks when the temperature goes over ninety degrees. But there has to be some connection between heart attacks and the cold as well. We just don't know what it is."

How Body Defenses Can Go Wrong

Heart disease involves more than the heart itself. The heart is the body's pump for circulating blood. The blood takes oxygen from the lungs and delivers it to the tissues by way of the circulatory system. This entire system is involved in heart disease and of course so is the blood that courses through it.

In Max's case, the cholesterol level of his blood was of concern to his cardiologist because cholesterol can very easily be deposited upon the walls of blood vessels. Researchers are not sure what causes it to be deposited in some people and not in others, but few doctors are willing to take chances. They feel that with a lower cholesterol level in the blood, there is less of a chance of the cholesterol being deposited. In addition, Max's blood vessels had lost their elasticity. He had arterio-sclerosis. This, too, was a problem.

The weather appeared to affect Max's cholesterol levels, but does it have an effect on other parts of the blood? I found that a number of researchers had investigated these areas and, as with all weather-related problems, there is a complex of interactions.

For example: Hemoglobin carries oxygen to the cells, and at high altitudes we need greater amounts of hemoglobin. The body manages this by producing more red blood cells, the hemoglobin carriers. These are formed in the bone marrow and stored in the spleen. High altitudes stimulate the bone marrow and spleen to release more cells, but seasonal changes in weather and daily pressure changes also cause ups and downs in the red-blood-cell count. So does the amount of adrenaline we release; adrenaline release is influenced by weather. The protein we eat forms the "globin" in hemoglobin, and we eat less protein in hot weather. The thyroid gland is weather sensitive, and it affects the bone-marrow production of red cells. And so it goes, one organ in the body affecting another—and the weather affecting all of them.

One of the body defenses can also turn around to become a body destroyer: the coagulation of blood. Its obvious purpose is to stop bleeding until the body can repair a wound.

Unfortunately, blood doesn't coagulate only when we want it to. It sometimes forms little clots inside the body for one reason or another, and these clots can come loose and be carried by the blood. A clot in the bloodstream can cause a stroke or death, depending on where it lodges. One of the many substances that go into blood clots is fibrinogen. Shortly after World War II, two physicians at the University of Freiburg—Drs. G. Caroli and J. Pichotka—discovered that blood clots more quickly before the passage of fronts and during thunderstorms. After the front passes, the blood clots at a normal rate.

This means that there is a greater possibility of a clot forming in the bloodstream just before a front passes over and during a thunderstorm. To the man or woman with no heart problem, there doesn't seem to be much danger. But if you are in the high-cardiac-risk group, it could be a very real danger.

What are the risk factors? High blood pressure is one. A high cholesterol or triglycerides level is another. A smoker is at risk, as is any male diabetic. If you have heart disease in your family, your risk is greater, and if you're obese, it's greater, too. Those people under stress—emotional stress, stress on the job, financial stress—are also in the high-risk category. If you have more than one of these symptoms, your risk factor goes up.

When I spoke to Dr. Ranscht-Froemsdorff of the Institute für Balneologie and Klimaphisiologie in Freiburg bout his work in sferics, he mentioned that these long electromagnetic waves caused an increase in blood clotting. He felt the increase was not significant, but that it might be significant to people at cardiac risk. Thunderstorms emit sferics, and his recent work confirmed the earlier studies of Drs. Caroli and Pichotka.

In addition to blood cells, hemoglobin, and the fibrinogen

in the blood, many other parts of the body are affected by weather and, in turn, affect the heart. The liver influences the proteins dissolved in the blood. The thyroid and adrenal glands affect the liver, and the weather has an effect on the thyroid and adrenals.

The hypothalamus, that complex regulating center in the brain, is much influenced by weather, and it indirectly controls the amount of salt in the blood. One of the first things a cardiologist will do if you show signs of incipient heart disease is to limit your salt intake. But this must be done carefully so the delicate salt balance of the body is not upset.

The weather also affects how we get rid of salt. Earlier I mentioned salt loss through sweating in extremely hot weather, but even a warm front will cause us to lose some salt. And cold fronts, too, affect the salt balance. When a cold front passes over, salt loss decreases. Since the salt levels are regulated by the hypothalamus, pituitary, adrenal, and thyroid—all weather sensitive organs—the weather's impact on the body's salt reserves is not surprising.

One way of determining the effect of weather on the heart is to see how many heart problems occur when the weather changes. Another method is to compare heart disease in different weathers. Dr. Helmuth Brezowski, director of a biometeorological unit in Bad Tölz in Germany, studied heart disease in 75,000 people. He compared the number of heart attacks occurring on warm, humid days with those occurring on cold, humid days and for all seasons of the year.

With acute cardiovascular disease and embolism, warm, humid weather is the real killer in every season.

With stroke, infarcts, and coronary insufficiency, warm, humid weather kills more in the summertime, but cold, humid weather kills more in the spring, fall, and winter.

Another correlation of heart disease with weather occurred during the summer of 1966 in New York City, when there was a 19 percent increase in deaths from heart disease. During July 1966 there were over 116,000: more than 28,000 extra deaths—a sizable number. The only weather element that paced this increase in death was temperature. For a week at the end of June it was in the high eighties. The death rate shot up one week later, in July.

Eighty degrees is not a high temperature for a New York summer. But the temperature rose into the eighties from the sixties in *one* day. The extra deaths may well have occurred among people who could not adapt to the sudden change. It wasn't the stress of heat as such, but the stress of the forced adaptation to more heat so very quickly, that did them in.

The same summer brought a similar increase in death to other cities in the United States. In Illinois a heat wave raised temperatures dramatically overnight to 89° along with a high humidity for a number of days. The combined heat and humidity caused a 36 percent increase in the death rate for people over sixty-five. There was also a significant increase in all heart-disease deaths. Again, it was not the heat but the sudden shift from low to high temperature early in the summer that caused the deaths.

A complicated interaction operates among all our body systems when there are extreme weather shifts in a short time. An extra strain is put on the body, and the weakest among us—those over sixty-five or those who are cardiac risks—are least likely to survive.

Not all of us are affected by the weather in the same way. An Israeli scientist, Dr. F. Dreyfus, studied the incidence of myocardial infarction in different communities in Israel. Although all the people he studied had lived in Israel in the same climate for many years, different groups were differently affected by heart disease, depending on where they came from.

The highest incidence was among Ashkenazic Jews from Eastern, Central, and Western Europe. The lowest was found in the oriental Jews from Yemen and the eastern Mediterranean. Other studies showed that the European Jews, between the ages of one and ten, had a greater degree of early problems with their coronary arteries than the orientals did. The doctor concluded that there was a strong ethnic factor at work.

In the United States, blacks seem more prone to high blood pressure than whites, even those who are living in the exact same socioeconomic conditions.

It was thought till recently that the difference was due to the greater psychological stress that blacks are under in our country. However, it may be due to the fact that their bodies retain salt, which aggravates high blood pressure.

Dr. Richard F. Gillun of the University of Minnesota Medical School in Minneapolis feels it may be an adaptive characteristic in their ancestors. In the African heat it would have been useful to conserve salt lost by perspiration. This would make their high blood pressure, with its extra risk of heart attacks, a genetic trait.

Dos and Don'ts

If you suffer from any type of heart disease, you should try to live in areas without any great atmospheric turbulence, at least during very hot and cold seasons. If you can't relocate during the dead of winter or the heat of summer, protect yourself. In winter, stay home on windy days and just before or after the passage of fronts. These are times to rest and take it easy. Air conditioning in the summer helps the cardiac patient, as does a warm, comfortable house in the winter.

Serious operations, especially heart operations, should be postponed if possible when the weather is disturbed.

Stay away from high altitudes if you have any heart problem. The difficulty of getting enough oxygen from the thin air only aggravates the heart.

Whether or not you are at cardiac risk, the ideal temperature for outdoor exercise, such as jogging, is between 40° and 60°. Jogging is often good exercise to help recovery from a heart attack, and you can jog comfortably in temperatures as low as 15°, if you watch the wind-chill factor and dress properly. At 20°, a 5-mile-an-hour wind will give you a chill equivalent to that of 15°.

In cold weather, if you are at risk, dress warmly—wear thermal underwear and a hat. A face mask for angina sufferers is a must.

If you are at cardiac risk, cut down on exercise when the temperature hits 80° and cut it out altogether when it reaches 85°. If the humidity is high, watch out.

When weather changes are rapid and extreme, the cardiac-risk patient should take it very easy and avoid any extra work or exertion.

Chapter Twelve

Aches and Pains
in Bones and Joints

When I first started my research for this book, I decided to go to Philadelphia to see Dr. Joseph Lee Hollander. I had read of Dr. Hollander's work and I respected him as a sound and sensible scientist. I had many questions about the weather's effect on health, and felt that if anyone could set me straight, it was he. I knew, too, that he had worked with a climate control chamber.

Dr. Hollander, a tall, balding man in his fifties, is professor of medicine at the University of Pennsylvania's School of Medicine and an authority on arthritis. The entrance to the climate control room was an oval door of reinforced steel with a small porthole. An adjoining wall held an array of dials and meters.

The chamber, he explained, was patterned on one built in Sweden thirty-five years ago. "When I first thought of building it, I was stopped by the cost. It would have been impossible, except for a brilliant engineer who worked with us for eight years. As it was, it came to one hundred twenty-five thousand dollars and most of that was from private donations."

"But what does it do?" I asked. "It looks like an air lock into a submarine or a space ship."

"I suppose it would do well under sea or in outer space. It's a little room about fifteen feet square and surrounded by re-inforced concrete walls and it has heavy plate-glass windows. Actually, it's a little apartment, with a bathroom, bed, chairs, bureau, table, radio, and telephone. You can be more comfortable there than in a hospital room."

"But who uses it?"

He led me back to his office and explained, "We selected arthritic patients from our practice and from our clinic, from the hospital and the general population, patients who claim that their symptoms get worse whenever there's a weather change. They were truly weather sensitive, and we asked them if they would volunteer to live in our special apartment for three or four weeks. We could offer them complete rest in a perfect climate at no charge."

"Did you have any takers?"

"Quite a few."

"What happened once they moved in?"

"We controlled the climate. The room has submarine doors and pressure equalizer valves. It's entirely sealed and we can change the barometric pressure inside, as well as the humidity, temperature, air ionization, and rate of air flow. We can give them any environment we wish. They had a phone inside. We brought them meals, gave them occupational therapy, nurses, doctors. It was a fine rest for them and we were able to experiment with weather changes.

"For the first week we kept everything constant to let them adjust to their new environment. Our first experiment was simple. With each patient, we changed one element of the climate. We either lowered or raised the air pressure. Then we changed the temperature, the humidity, the air flow, the ionization, and we did it at random, one element at a time."

"What happened?"

He shrugged. "Nothing. Not one of the changes produced any consistent effect on their symptoms."

I sat down uneasily, seeing the entire theory of weather sensitivity shaken. "Then you're saying that the weather has no effect on arthritis."

"Of course it has. I'm saying that, unlike our experiment, the weather doesn't vary one element at a time. You get a change in temperature and with it a change in humidity, or in pressure, or all three will change."

"I see. What did you do next?"

"We changed two factors. When we dropped the pressure and at the same time raised the humidity, we got quite a reaction from our patients. Seven out of eight who had rheumatoid arthritis felt worse, and so did three out of four who had osteoarthritis. The unusual thing about it was that we could observe their symptoms. We could see the change when we checked their joints. We could notice that all the elements they told us were getting worse, were really worse."

"How long did it take them in the climate control chamber before they began to feel uncomfortable?"

"They felt bad about four hours after we had changed the humidity and the pressure, and by six to eight hours our physical examination showed us that they were in bad shape. But it was the simultaneous change in both barometric pressure and humidity, and not the high humidity or low pressure alone, that did it."

"Why, out of all the possible weather elements, did you choose those two factors, low barometric pressure and high humidity, to start with?"

He shrugged. "Those are the two prevailing factors in nature before any rainstorm, and that's the time when most arthritics complain about their symptoms. You must understand that weather effect is not just an old wives' tale, not when we can duplicate it here and actually observe our patient's reaction."

Dr. Hollander and his associates have used sophisticated methods to demonstrate what most arthritic patients know. In fact, back in 1879 a Chicago doctor, J. T. Everett, reported that after observing many cases of arthritis for over twelve years he found that when stormy weather brought a falling barometer and a rising humidity, all his patients began complaining. The closer the storm and the quicker it came, the worse the pain and the louder the complaints.

Other researchers in the early years of this century, physicians aware of the connection between weather and arthritis, began adding up the odd facts about arthritis that had always been considered folklore. In one study at the Mayo Clinic, almost four hundred patients suffering from arthritis were observed and questioned over an entire year. They were asked about their symptoms every day before the barometric pressure was recorded for that day. Since they were questioned before the pressure was taken, neither they nor the questioners knew what the forecast was. Accordingly, they wouldn't be influenced in explaining their symptoms.

The researchers found that 72 percent of the time the patients felt increasing pain when the barometer fell and relief when it rose. Before and during the storm their pain increased. In fine, sunny weather their pain decreased.

Other studies around the country brought out the fact that warm and cold fronts, with their shifting barometric pressures, also cause arthritic pain.

My Neighbor, the Walking Barometer

In this last finding, the scientists are way behind my neighbor in the country. She is a walking barometer. At seventy-two, Anita is still going strong, but bent almost double with arthritis. A woman with a good sense of humor and a passionate gardener, Anita laughs at her own troubles. "So I'm bent over. I'm nearer to the ground, and it's easier for me to weed.

And I'll tell you what; I can tell any weather change better than that funny guy on television."

Bending down beside her to help her weed, I asked, "How do you tell?"

"It's a matter of pain." Sitting back on her heels, she sighed. "I hurt like the devil before the weather is going to change. It's not just an all-over hurt, but it's very sharp, very much in one place—my hands."

Looking at me keenly, she added, "And I'll tell you this though you might laugh at me. If it's a cold day, and I get that stabbing pain, I know that in three hours—exactly three hours—it's going to turn warm. I know it as sure as I'm breathing."

"Can you predict the cold, too?"

"Yes. No matter how warm a day, when the pain hits my hands, I say to myself, 'Anita—give it eight hours and it's going to turn cold.' There may be a storm, too; but you can count on the cold."

"What do you do?"

"There's not much I can do, but I know enough to take it easy. I cut down on anything physical. You have to learn to live with arthritis. You have to learn your limitations and how far you can go. My body sends me a message that no doctor can equal." She glanced at me slyly. "I have to read weather language."

I asked a rheumatologist of my acquaintance about Anita's acute weather sensitivity, expecting her to laugh. But instead she nodded seriously. "Yes. Weather language is what it is. Most arthritics have that ability, though some are not aware of it. The weather has such a direct effect on them that they become what the Germans call *wettervögel*—weather birds. They can tell us when a warm front or a cold front passes over, and they can tell it in advance. I have one patient who can tell me exactly how severe any storm is going to be, and always well in advance of that storm."

"What exactly is arthritis?"

She laughed. "How can I be exact about such a disease? Its symptoms are so different in different people. Let me see. Strictly speaking, arthritis is an inflammation of a joint. When it's acute, the joint becomes painful, hot sometimes when you touch it, even red and swollen. That's the acute form, but arthritis can also be chronic. Then we call it rheumatoid arthritis. There are changes in the membranes around the joints and in the joints themselves. The bones often degenerate— but not always. It's a complicated disease."

"And what's the difference between arthritis and rheumatism?"

"We tend to lump them both together. Rheumatism is usually an inflammation of the muscles and joints, and it's a painful disease too. It's hard to separate it from arthritis, if indeed there is a separation. But they both react to weather in the same way."

"But why?" I asked. "What element in the weather does it?"

She looked up at the ceiling. "If we knew that . . . I suppose, and it's my own theory, that it's the fact that our body joints are closed containers that does it. When the pressure is low, they expand, and that causes pain. But that's about as far as I can go."

My friend's theory is a common one. But it's just that, a theory. It has never been proved. Measuring the expansion of a person's joints under low pressure, or their contraction under high pressure, is almost impossible. But proof of this theory comes from other sources. A report from the United States Navy notes that when navy divers had to go down under high pressure, any arthritic pain in their joints disappeared.

We think of navy divers as healthy young men who should be free of arthritis, but health, like youth, is a matter of where you stand. Many of the divers were in their thirties, and arthritic changes can start early in life. They may not become troublesome enough to notice until we're forty or fifty, but the changes are there.

The relief felt by the divers continued for a long time afterwards. It seems to indicate that putting joints under pressure helps to relieve pain, just as their expansion in low-pressure systems seems to cause pain.

In Sweden, Dr. G. Erdstrom, who developed the original controlled climate chamber on which Dr. Hollander patterned his, treated his arthritic patients by putting them into the chamber and creating a warm, dry atmosphere under high barometric pressure. He treated seven arthritics this way. Four of these, he reported, were cured, but seven patients are hardly enough to prove anything.

What is needed is a number of sensible studies such as Dr. Hollander's in Philadelphia. Most rheumatologists that I have talked to are aware of his work. The attitude of a rheumatologist attached to Lenox Hill Hospital with a tremendous practice in New York City is typical of most practitioners.

"Yes, indeed," he agreed, "the weather has a tremendous impact—on some people. I have patients who go to pieces before a thunderstorm. Their bones ache, their scars trouble them, and every arthritic process acts up. But I have other patients, just as bad off, who don't seem affected at all by any weather condition. What can I do about it anyway? Tell them to get in out of the pressure or lack of pressure? No. I use drugs to treat my patients because I can rely on drugs. I can calibrate the dosage and treat each one individually according to his need. You must remember that arthritics are very different. No two of them are alike."

I became aware of the truth of that—no two arthritics are alike—as I investigated the effect weather had on health. Not only are no two arthritics alike, but no two people are alike. No two people speak the same weather language. Everyone reacts differently to the weather, which is what weather sensitivity is all about.

In Freiburg, Dr. Harflinger told me that 30 percent of all people are weather sensitive. Another doctor who had done research in the field had another view.

"I see it as a spectrum," he said. "All of us, to some degree, are sensitive to the weather. Some of us are extremely sensitive; others react to it very little, but they do react. Between these two extremes there is a vast range of weather sensitivity. It's true that Dr. Harflinger's thirty percent lies to one side of that range, but it doesn't mean that the rest of us do not feel the weather. It simply means that when the weather gets bad, we are either not aware of what troubles us, or we are able to overcome that trouble, to cope with it, or, in a few cses, the troubling symptoms are not enough to bother us."

I agree with this "spectrum" view of weather sensitivity, and from other conversations with other rheumatologists, I'm sure that most arthritics also respond over a spectrum. Between the highly weather-sensitive arthritic and the nearly totally unreactive one, there is an enormous number of arthritic sufferers who are affected to some extent by weather changes. If you are one of these, there are some things you can do to help yourself.

Dos and Don'ts

Much of the biometeorological research about weather and arthritis seems to indicate that arthritics are troubled by damp, cold weather, two elements that are relatively easy to control. On cold, rainy days, stay indoors, dry and warm. If you must go out, bundle up against the cold. Use an umbrella and be sure your boots and outer clothes are waterproof.

Try not to be physically active when there is a weather change. This is a time to take it easy. Physical activity simply strains the arthritic joints.

If you do get cold and wet, try to warm up your body as soon as you can. A warm bath is great. Heat of any kind helps.

If the weather is particularly bad, and nothing seems to help you, try compresses. Wet towels will do, alternately warm and cold. Apply to the painful area, but be sure to end up with warm.

Be aware of stress. Any kind of stress—your job, your family, and of course the weather—can increase your pain. If you are under stress, understand what is causing it. Don't blame it on yourself. That just increases the stress. Put the blame where it belongs, on the weather if necessary.

Arthritis sufferers do worse when humidity is high. If they have a choice, they should live in a dry, warm, sunny climate with little air turbulence. However, many rheumatologists caution that if you move just for the climate, the stress of moving and relocating may outweigh any benefits the climate gives.

One doctor told me of a patient who had been visiting Arizona for a number of years for two- or three-week periods. While he was there he felt that his arthritis was better. Last year he moved there permanently, and in eight weeks he called his doctor to ask that all his medical records be sent to Phoenix. He felt that his arthritis was worse than it had ever been.

Why did this happen? According to the doctor, two or three weeks was not long enough to find out if the climate could really improve his condition. Nor had he stopped to consider the other problems of relocation—the job market, friends, re-adjustment of his wife and children, and his own ties to the home he had left.

For most arthritic sufferers weather should not be the sole factor in relocating. However, one benefit was reported by a woman badly crippled with arthritis who had moved to a dry, warm area. "The pain of taking heavy clothes off during cold weather, buttoning coats, and pulling on boots, was more than I could stand. I used to stay indoors rather than go out most of the winter. When my husband retired, we moved out here and I've never regretted it."

Finally, since we all react differently to weather, see if you can learn to understand weather language and match your aches and pains to the changes as shown in the charts in Chapter Two.

You will gain an awareness of your own weather sensitivity, and a clue to managing it.

Chapter Thirteen

Cancer: Is Weather a Factor?

In the course of collecting data on weather-related diseases, I found that many cancer patients had one surprising factor in common, their birth date. Mary Ann is typical. In her late fifties, Mary Ann has had two mastectomies for breast cancer and has passed the critical five-year period without a recurrence. "They tell me I'm home free now," she smiled. "At least the cancer hasn't spread. They seem to have caught it in time." Mary Ann is tall, slim, and still a good-looking woman. She has taken her problem in stride and hasn't let it destroy her life.

"What struck me as fascinating," she said, "was the coincidence of birthdays when I was in the hospital."

"What do you mean?"

"Well, there were ten of us on the same floor, all with some sort of cancer or another, and all very hopeful about our chances of survival. We became very friendly, and we formed a little club, promising to keep in touch after we got out. We did too, and I still get long Christmas letters from six of them, the ones who have survived. We send birthday cards to each other. The funny thing is, of those ten, four were born in January. Isn't that a strange coincidence? It almost makes me believe in the influence of the stars."

"Why the stars?" I asked. "Why not the months?"

January: The Dangerous Month

I was troubled by Mary Ann's coincidence, until I came across the work of Dr. W.J.J. Sauvage Nolting. Dr. Nolting is a psychiatrist at Zeist in the Netherlands and, like many psychiatrists, he is intrigued by biometeorology. He examined the months in which cancer patients were born and discovered that more were born in the winter than at other times. Five years later he repeated his study, this time examining the birth records of over 15,000 cancer patients. He zeroed in on January as the month in which a disproportionate number of cancer victims was born.

"It didn't seem to matter what type of cancer we studied," Dr. Nolting said. "Breast cancer, intestinal cancer, even pulmonary cancer—January was the significant month."

Other researchers, curious about these findings, repeated this type of study in other countries and came up with the same fact. Cancer victims have a higher percentage of January births. There had to be some factor present in January that was not around for the rest of the year. Obviously that factor is cold.

Was it because the weather was cold at the time of their birth, or while they were still in the womb? If the cause was their birth during a cold month, you might reason that the cold affected their nutrition or their mother's milk and in this way started a chain of physiological events that would eventually lead to cancer in later years.

If the cold affected them while they were yet unborn, the

subsequent cancer could be due to a developmental problem. The growing embryo might have been affected by the mother's reaction to cold, by her dietary deficiency, or by the stress of the weather.

The correlation that Dr. Nolting discovered in Holland held true for many other countries, even for Australia in the Southern Hemisphere. But there the greatest number of cancer patients were born in July, Australia's coldest month! Again, cold seemed to be the significant factor, but how did the cold affect the babies?

We don't know the answer yet, but a number of studies seem to indicate a connection between cold and cancer. Drs. R. H. Fuller, E. Brown, and C. A. Mills, reporting in a scientific journal on the growth of cancer in mice, claimed that cancer grew more rapidly in low temperatures (55° to 64°) than at normal temperatures.

Another study, by a Virginia scientist, Dr. S. Krasnow, investigated the effect of chilling temperatures on cancer. Assuming that January was the coldest month in the United States, he compared the death rates from cancer with the daily temperature. He used the tweny-five counties with the highest cancer death rates and the twenty-five with the lowest death rates, and studied the wind-chill factor in those counties over a four-year period.

He found a significant connection between death from cancer and the chilling effect of wind and low temperature. There were more deaths from cancer of the lungs when the temperature dropped and the wind rose.

Could the added shock of cold weaken the breathing system of people suffering from cancer and send them over the edge? Since he was comparing deaths from cancer, not new cases of cancer, all the people who died probably had cancer already. The numbing effect of the cold on their systems may have been more than they could take.

Any strenuous exercise may also have been too much for them. In cold weather we work hard to keep going. We expend more energy, burn up more calories, and stress our bodies more. The people Dr. Krasnow studied, however, had cancer before they were exposed to the cold. Can the cold hurt us if we haven't got cancer? Can the cold be a factor in developing cancer? Could the cold that Dr. Nolting's babies experienced at birth increase their chances of cancer in later years? More biometeorological research may tell us.

There are two different ways in which any weather element, including cold, works on the body—directly and indirectly. One indirect method would be through the hormonal system. If extreme cold puts a stress on the hypothalamus, and this in turn activates other glands and causes them to turn out an excess of hormones, these extra hormones might have a role in producing cancer. We know that in women over a certain age an excess of the female hormone estrogen is somehow related to breast cancer. This is why, when a breast is removed for cancer, the surgeon will often remove the ovaries as well, to cut down on the body's natural production of estrogen.

However, the cold at the time of birth may not have been the villain in the piece. The children Dr. Nolting studied were born in January, but they were conceived in April of the previous year. By July certain critical parts of the fetal brain were forming. It is conceivable that the hot temperatures of July and August, the radiation of the sun, or some other meteorological disturbance might throw a monkey wrench into nature's careful management of the fetus. We know there is a link between cancer and DNA, the blueprint of life, and if the baby's DNA was disturbed, might not this lead to cancer in later years?

Again, the third month is the time when the hypothalamus, pituitary, and other glands are forming. Light and darkness have a profound effect on these organs, and the long summer days may upset the fetus. Whatever the reason, Dr. Nolting says, the result of all his work is a big boost for family planning: "*If all children in the Northern Hemisphere who are prone to cancer were born during the favorable summer months, seven to eleven percent fewer cancer cases could be anticipated.*"

The possible impact of the weather on the fetus in terms of cancer is reminiscent of the impact of heat in terms of birth defects mentioned earlier. Again, the same time, the third month of pregnancy is involved, and quite possibly the same factors—excessive heat or a lack of protein in the diet because of the heat.

But if this type of weather is a factor, it is only that—*one* factor in a disease that has dozens of possible factors as its cause.

Can the Sun Cause Cancer?

Ted is in his mid-fifties, but he looks younger. He has a trim build, all his hair—even though its sandy color is mixed with gray—and brilliant blue eyes. "Paul Newman eyes," his wife calls them fondly, "and they look perfect with his tan."

Ted doesn't regard tanning as a competitive sport. To him it's an important part of his job. "Hey, I'm a salesman, and I have an image to project. The clothes I wear, the way I watch my weight—it's all part of my business. My tan is important too. It impresses clients. They say, this guy is tanned even in winter. He can afford Florida, the islands, he must be on the ball."

The truth is, Ted can't afford going south for the winter. He spends every free hour in his backyard with a reflector or he slips into the park on his lunch hour to get an extra dose of sunlight.

Because of Ted's intense concentration on keeping fit, it was a terrible shock to him when his doctor told him that little black spot on his cheek was skin cancer. "We can remove it surgically and get a pretty decent-looking repair, but no more sun!

"Fair-skinned blonds with blue eyes have no business getting so much sun," the doctor cautioned. "You've got to learn that, even if it means changing your entire way of life. You were lucky this time. The next cancer might not be so easy to remove."

Does excess sunlight cause skin cancer? Was Ted's doctor right, or would Ted have developed cancer anyway? All the evidence seems to point to ultraviolet light as a cause. Certainly heredity plays an important part, maybe the most important. Some people won't get skin cancer no matter how much sun they get. Others seem prone to it with even a moderate amount. In Ireland, those Irish who are red-haired with the typical redhead's complexion and who tend to burn instead of tan are most liable to get skin cancer. Yet the Scandinavians, with fair skin and blond hair, have a low incidence of skin cancer. Of course, there is also very little direct sunlight in Scandinavia, but the chance of skin cancer goes up when the Scandinavian comes south and is overexposed to the sun.

Skin color plays an important role in all of this. Blacks get less skin cancer than whites. Studies in India show that fair-skinned people who come to live there have a ten-times-larger chance of getting skin cancer than the darker Indians. There is more skin cancer in the tropics than in temperate climates.

The team of Dr. B. S. Mackie, a dermatologist, and his wife, Leila E. Mackie, from Australia, set out to find some answer to the sun-cancer puzzle. The Mackies live in a sunlit land with a population heavy with transplanted Irish and English. It also has a high incidence of skin cancer.

Some facts they started with were that skin cancer almost always strikes the exposed parts of the body—the hands, arms, face, and neck. Sportsmen and outdoor laborers are more prone to skin cancer than office workers. It also strikes people with little or no melanin.

Part of Australia lies near the tropics and the sun's rays there are more intense since they strike horizontally. In the far north of the world, where skin cancer is infrequent, the sun's rays strike vertically and are less intense.

This is all circumstantial evidence, and although we may suspect the sun on the basis of these reports, we can't definitely convict it. The Mackies got harder evidence from microscopic examination of the skin of people exposed to excess sunlight, especially those with little or no pigment. "There are degenerative changes that eventually lead to skin cancer as we get older," they reported, and added that the less pigment there was in the skin, the more quickly cancer developed. But even adolescents, they warned, if they have no pigment, showed these changes.

If you are fair-skinned and exposed to a great deal of sunlight, watch for the skin changes that herald cancers. Of the three types, the most common is the Bora-cell cancer, which starts as a small pearly nodule slowly changing to a lump or ulcer. It usually appears on the face or neck.

The second—squamous-cell cancer of the skin—begins as a pink or white elevated lump with ulcers in the center. The rarest skin cancer is malignant melanoblastoma. It starts as a blackish area in a brownish freckle.

The work of the Mackies and others offers clear-cut proof that sunlight can cause skin cancer, but there is still some controversy about which is more important, heredity or sunlight. Whatever the cause, avoiding unnecessary sunburn, especially if you're fair-skinned, is a good precaution.

Calcium, Smog, and Danger Towns

Some Russian experimenters turned up a curious connection between cancer and the mind. They made a group of mice neurotic with continual electric shocks and disturbing noises. They then exposed those neurotic mice, along with a group of normal mice, to cancer-producing substances. The neurotic rodents developed tumors much more readily than the well-adjusted ones. The investigators decided that stress, whether emotional or physical, was a definite factor in causing cancer in animals.

In the United States, a number of statistical studies confirm this connection. In humans, emotional stress may accelerate cancer growth. From this it's a step, even if a giant one, to the conclusion that since there are climates that put stress on humans, these climates are a factor in aggravating cancer. Extreme heat or cold, excessive humidity, and even air turbulence could be causative agents.

This line of reasoning may seem far-fetched, but there is some more down-to-earth evidence that weather has something to do with how likely we are to get cancer.

Weather extremes affect the body's calcium level. Cancerous tissue has a relatively low calcium content. This lack of calcium can affect the cancer cells' ability to adhere to other cells. They tend to become loose and drift to other parts of the body if calcium is lacking. There they form new patches of cancer (metastases).

Although this fact is of interest to researchers, it would be foolish to try to apply it to cancer treatment, just as foolish as it would be to think that simply because you were born in January, you therefore have a greater chance of getting cancer. Too many other factors are implicated, in addition to weather: heredity, emotional stress, diet, drugs, radiation, and all the cancer-causing insults your body has absorbed since birth, from food additives to environmental pollution, from cigarette smoking to traumatic injury. There is no end to the possible causes of cancer, so there is no way to "play it safe." The best you can do is avoid some known cancer causes, such as tobacco smoke and smog.

One cause of cancer may, to a small degree, be psychological, in the mind, but another cause we are much more certain about is in the air. Weather, with its vagrant winds and temperature inversions, causes us to be exposed to heavy doses of carcinogenic substances.

Consider the summer of 1978, when the temperature in Los Angeles rose to a record high of 114°. Accompanying the heat was a temperature inversion over the city. The sky turned an orange yellow. For days people breathed the heavy oppressive smog. Doubtless the deaths from cancer caused by that smog will be numerous and will occur over many years.

Heart patients and stroke victims were warned by the city to avoid exertion. Unfortunately no one suggested that heavy smokers stay home, or that asthma sufferers take it easy, or that people who worked in factories and were usually exposed to smog should take extra precautions during this time.

A close relationship between cancer and smog has been found all over the world. In England cancer deaths are highest in smog-bound cities. In the Netherlands, the prime danger zones are the sites of large air-polluting chemical industries. And in the United States heavy smog areas have also been linked to increased cancer deaths. The connection seems more and more obvious as more and more areas are studied. And inasmuch as studies with animals have already proved that smog itself, in controlled experiments, causes cancer, we know the weather indirectly and smog directly as two causes of cancer.

Polluted air is only one of the many causes of cancer. An environmental study came up with the startling conclusion that there is more cancer among people living in places where the ground tends to be wet because of proximity to streams of running water. Is there such a thing as a cancer zone, an area where one is more liable to get cancer?

A Maryland physician, Dr. William Chen, studied every cancer case in the past fifty years in a 300-square-mile area. He found that the incidence of cancer was much higher than expected in certain places. He speculated that radioactive soil might be the cause. There might be many reasons why these areas report more cancer cases.

In New Jersey in recent years clusters of cancer in children were found. One area suffers an incidence of cancer far above the national average. The cause? None has yet been found. One might ask whether the investigators checked the weather patterns over the cancer zones. Are there any winds from radioactive areas? Any radioactive tailings in the ground? Any fallout in distant watersheds that could lead to contaminated wells?

And what of the birth dates of the children stricken?

There are many possible factors, and many that may depend on the weather and its vagaries.

Dos and Don'ts

Since there is no conclusive research on the connection between cancer and birth dates or extreme cold or emotional stress, there is little advice that can be given to cancer patients or the rest of us who fear we may become cancer victims. We should pressure our congressmen to allot more money for research, earmarking some of it for studies about weather factors that seem to affect cancer-prone people.

For the rest of us, it would help if we were made aware of the dangers that threaten when winds and temperature inversions cause us to be exposed to cancer-causing material. Radio and television stations should broadcast more detailed reports to alert us to the dangers of cancer-causing pollutants.

Chapter Fourteen

Allergies, Respiratory Diseases, and the Weather

In the 1930s I had a close friend, a young woman in her teens, full of vitality and very eager to get everything out of life.

"I have to," Ruth told me intently. "I haven't that much longer to live."

"What are you talking about?" I asked, embarrassed at such depth of feeling.

"I've got tuberculosis. My mother died of it when she was still in her thirties. I don't want to go through a marriage and three kids only to leave them when they're babies, like she did. I don't care if I die soon. I want to get the most out of whatever time I have!"

Ruth died a few years later, and perhaps she lived those years as intensely as she wanted to. I don't know. I just know that two months after she told me about her illness, I talked to her again, and she said that the doctors had insisted that she get out of the city and up to a high altitude.

"They have a place picked out, a sanitarium up at Lake Placid, and they say it will help me, maybe cure me."

"Are you going?"

She shook her head, her eyes untroubled. "Not me! The hell with being stuck away in some ice-bound sanitarium in the mountains. I'd just as soon go to prison."

Those were the days before antibiotics effective against tuberculosis had been discovered. Today a tuberculosis sufferer can stay in almost any climate and, with treatment, recover. As a result, tuberculosis is on the decline. Because we hardly ever hear of it, we have forgotten how deadly it—like diphtheria and smallpox—can be. And yet newspapers not infreqeuntly report outbreaks of tuberculosis and the measures taken to overcome them.

There is little doubt that before the drug that cured tuberculosis was discovered, weather played an important role in the progress of the disease. In northern countries, more people suflered from it in the spring. When the weather grew warmer, fewer people were cured. The best results of therapy came in winter when there was little sun and a great deal of cold.

Why cold has such an effect on tuberculosis has never been explained, but one theory that makes sense is that the cold causes the body's metabolism to speed up. This heightened metabolism helps the body fight off the tubercular infection.

Another explanation of why cold stress, so deadly in other diseases, should be helpful in the treatment of TB suggested that since patients were well fed and warmly dressed, some of the bad effects of cold stress were eliminated. Patients did have to fight for their breath in the thin mountain air, and this struggle helped strengthen their weakened lungs.

Physicians are no longer sure that this extra work is all that good. There seems no logical reason to put a sanitarium up in the mountains. According to biometeorologists, the best location for it is a dry place. Humidity is bad for lung problems. Pine forests, doctors say, are helpful, because of the negative ions found there. Pine forests also keep sunlight away from the patients, and solar radiation may be harmful to TB sufferers. This may be why the poorest rate of cure was found in the spring when the sunlight increased. Perhaps the cold wasn't a dominant factor!

Air turbulence, winds, and fronts are bad for the tubercular patient. They make breathing more difficult. Of course any chemical pollution is an added insult. Climate therapy, which used to be the mainstay of tuberculosis treatment, has fallen off in popularity in the United States, although it is still used as a supplement to antibiotic therapy in Europe. However, climate therapy is also important in treating a number of other lung diseases besides tuberculosis, such as asthma and emphysema.

Emphysema is widespread in the United States, no doubt because of the prevalence of cigarette smoking, one of its main causes. It consists of a gradual deterioration of the little air sacs in the lungs, and cannot be cured. As the disease progresses, the lungs become less and less able to absorb oxygen from the air; eventually the victim chokes to death. But weather, the proper kind of weather, can delay the process and add years to the victim's life.

Unpolluted air and low humidity help. Humid air makes it harder for the lungs to absorb oxygen, and pollution can irritate the lungs. Many emphysema patients go west, to places where the air is dry and unpolluted. Unhappily the desert air can also interfere with breathing because of the dust that it carries.

Biometeorologists suggest that the best place for anyone suffering from emphysema—or asthma—is the lee side of a mountain, not high enough for altitude to be a problem, but a good distance above sea level. The eastern slopes of the Rocky Mountains or the Sierra Nevadas are ideal.

How to Help Asthmatics

Tuberculosis has a frightening sound, and emphysema is a killer, but asthma seems like a mild disease—so many children have it. And yet asthma too can be a killer, and asthma is closely linked to the weather.

A study in Canada compared the weather in Montreal and Toronto with the intensity of asthma attacks. Asthmatics, the Canadians found, were at their worst on foggy, smoky, or hazy days, during thunderstorms, and whenever the weather was turbulent.

A study in the German Democratic Republic made a similar point. Dr. Hans Blaha, medical director of the Volkssolbad in Bad Salzungen, was able to match weather conditions against breathing difficulties in 15,000 asthmatic patients. Over half had their attacks in cold and rainy weather; one-fifth had attacks during any change of weather, and one-eighth in foggy, muggy, or hot weather. Almost all improved when the weather changed.

The weather had such a strong effect, Dr. Blaha believes, because it damages the lining of the nasopharynx. The asthmatics secreted too much mucus and blocked their air passages. Getting them out of the humid air was tremendously helpful, Dr. Blaha decided. Sometimes merely changing where they lived or worked did the trick. The change didn't have to be dramatic, he noted. Even moving to another part of the city might do it.

If an asthmatic couldn't move, Dr. Blaha suggested changing the temperature and humidity in home or office. "An air conditioner to dry out the air would be a good thing."

Death from asthma, and from bronchitis too, is twice as high in cities as in the country. In the children's book *Heidi*, Clara is sent to live with Heidi in the mountains, and she becomes healthy and well. Clara is cured by "plenty of goat's milk and the healthy air." Probably the goat's milk didn't help, but she was right about the air. High altitude stimulates the endocrine system, which causes beneficial hormones to flow through the body. The high altitude also contains pure air, no city pollutants, and less humidity to start mucus flowing. And of course the thinner air causes the body to work harder breathing, which helps to develop the chest muscles.

Another possible reason for the healthful effects of a mountain climate might be the ions found there. As a rule they are negative ions, which, if Soviet reports are true, are of benefit in any breathing problem. At least certain famous spas, such as the one at Biarritz, are supposed to offer more negative than positive ions in the air.

Researchers are not sure that ions help; they *are* sure that pollutants hurt. Take the case of Clarence. Back in 1945 after his return from Europe with the American army, Clarence decided to stay in the service.

"I wanted to see some more of the world and I had a chance to get to Japan. In those days an army officer in Japan had it made. I was stationed not far from Yokohama, in the Kanto Plain, and I had a beautiful house and a lovely Japanese lady to look after me—in all ways. I spent five great years, and then it hit me. The worst kind of asthma. We called it Yokohama Asthma. I could hardly breathe

"The doctors at the dispensary kept after me about my previous history of asthma, but hell, I had no previous history. I had never had it before. Sure, I was a big smoker then, but that's all, and I was young, just thirty. It went on for a long time. I wheezed and coughed, and finally they sent me home. And I wasn't the only one. Our dispensary was flooded with guys suffering from the same thing. It cleared up the moment I hit the boat, and it hasn't bothered me since."

The only clues the army ever found to Yokohama Asthma was a temperature inversion over the Kanto Plain area, and a nearby polluting industrial setup. This type of asthma has since been called pollution asthma, and has occurred in many other places. In New Orleans pollution asthma was connected with wind patterns, inversions, and fires burning in nearby dumps. In Nashville, a direct link was found between pollution asthma and sulfur dioxide in the air.

In Brisbane, Australia, another cause of asthma, pollen, was also tied to the weather. Dr. E. H. Derrick of the Queensland Institute of Medical Research found that in the six cool months of the Australian year, asthma rates rose one or two months after the temperature rose. The reason, Dr. Derrick decided, was the growth of pollen-producing grasses. Warm temperature started them. A month later they came into flower and released their pollen, to the misery of all asthma sufferers. When the temperature rose above 70° the asthma attacks stopped because at this temperature the plants stopped producing pollen.

But perhaps more important than pollen or pollution is the weather itself. A recent report from Japan indicates that they have been able to control some of the industrial pollution, such as that over the Kanto Plain in the fifties, but they cannot control the weather's effect on asthma. Dr. R. Mimoto, from the Kochi Mimoto Hospital, has been observing bronchial asthma for more than two years in Kochi city.

Bronchial asthma is an asthmatic disease caused by an allergic reaction to an irritating substance. Dr. Mimoto found that it decreases in the summer, when stable high atmospheric pressure sets in. He told a recent meeting of the International Biometeorological Society that in the other seasons it varies with the changes in atmospheric pressure, fronts, air temperature, and humidity.

The important element he stressed, is *change* itself. And other studies have shown the same. A change in the weather—whether from good to bad or bad to good, hot to cold or cold to hot—upsets the human breathing apparatus.

Bronchial asthma may not hit at the time of a weather change; it often comes as much as a week later. A London physician, J. T. Boyd, reported in the *Proceedings of the Royal Society of Medicine* a close association between deaths from respiratory disease in people over forty-five and the temperature and humidity of the week before.

He also discovered that more people died when the weather dipped below freezing and there was a thick fog in the air. "When you get this kind of weather—cold and foggy—there is an increase of polluting sulfur dioxide. Breathing it in with the fog forces the sulfur dioxide to change to a caustic, hydrosulfuric acid. The damage to the throat and chest from this acid can cause enough irritation to pave the way to a severe attack of bronchitis or asthma."

Other studies seem to pinpoint the fog alone as the real troublemaker. Two British researchers writing in the British medical journal *Lancet* said, "In a stable group of men there are wide, wide variations in disabling lung diseases, and the variations can't be explained by social, economic, or occupational factors, or by any other consistent differences in climate *other than fog*." Again, the medically accusing finger is pointed.

A Weather Clue to Allergies

There seems to be a relationship among asthma, bronchial asthma, and bronchitis, on the one hand, and allergies on the other. Allergy-producing substances, such as pollen or smog, can irritate asthmatics and bronchitis sufferers. The body may react in similar ways; however, the mechanism that causes each reaction is different. Allergic reactions are really body defenses gone askew. The machinery intended to protect us upsets us, and we become hypersensitive. A list of the natural and artificial substances that set some of us off sneezing, wheezing, coughing, or breaking out in rashes and hives would be endless. Certainly it includes molds, spores, bacteria, toxic plants like poison ivy, any kind of food, and all sorts of other potential irritants.

Evelyn, a young married businesswoman, has a terrible

allergy to dust. "I keep a spotless house, even though it means hassling myself all week long. My husband is a slob and no real help, but if there's even a trace of dust I go off into a terrible attack of sneezing. The funny thing is, I took all kinds of tests and they all came out negative for house dust. The doctors couldn't find the slightest allergic response. Don, my husband, was delighted. He said it's all in my head, and I've got a psychological masochistic streak. I love to clean. But that's not true. I *know* I react to dust."

Evelyn went from doctor to doctor before she finally found one who had an idea about the true cause of her allergy.

"Is it any worse when the humidity is bad?" he asked.

Surprised, Evelyn shrugged. "I don't know. Humidity doesn't bother me."

At the doctor's urging, Evelyn kept a log of her allergic attacks and matched it against the humidity. To her surprise, there was a perfect correlation. She had her attacks only when the weather was humid. "The culprit," the pleased allergist explained, "is not house dust per se."

"What do you mean 'per se'?"

"I mean," he told her, "that humidity allows certain fungi to develop."

"And I'm allergic to them?"

"No, but they break down the house dust. Dust is made up primarily of wood, paper, and fabric; the fungus breaks it down and changes it, and you're allergic to one of those resulting elements."

Evelyn might still be shuttling from doctor to doctor or she might have accepted her husband's diagnosis of psychological masochism if this allergist hadn't established the connection between humidity and her allergy.

For Evelyn it was the humidity factor—for others it might be heat, weather fronts, even barometric pressure. Almost anything can cause an allergic attack, just as an allergic attack can take any form. It can show up as an asthmatic reaction, a runny nose, hay fever, a rash, hives, itching, stomach upsets, nausea, and on and on. They once called syphilis the great imitator because it mimicked so many other diseases, but surely today's allergies deserve that title.

Probably the worst and most persistent cause of allergic reactions is pollen, any sort of pollen. But some very allergic sufferers are at their worst from the middle of September to the end of October, and all known pollens are on their way out during this time. Even molds are rare then. The usual explanation has been, "Well, vacation is over and you're just allergic to work," or to the newly painted apartment you've come back to, or to the city, or country, or whatever.

Careful examination of these allergic people seems to indicate that not only isn't pollen the problem; other allergens are probably not to blame either. They have an allergic reaction to weather itself! Their symptoms follow a period of quiet atmospheric conditions, usually under high pressure. After a series of cold fronts with rain, thunderstorms, and even hail, the relative humidity goes up, and their allergies come out. The impact of all this weather on the body can yield a number of results. Cold, for example, brings an increase in the activity of the thyroid and other glands. It affects the way we use oxygen and may cause spasms in the lungs. It also affects the hypothalamus, the regulator of so many body functions.

Cold may also trigger the antigen-antibody system of the body and produce all kinds of allergic responses, from asthma to body rashes, from itching to attacks of sneezing. When this happens, it does no good to place the blame on psychological factors or to search for pollen, dust, or molds. The cause is the weather.

Hazel's case is typical. An old friend, she came to visit us one day with red blotches on her hands and face. "I don't know what it is," she told us. "I didn't even know I had it at first."

"How did it happen?" my wife asked.

"I got on the bus yesterday—you know, it was cold and

windy, and I noticed that the woman across from me kept staring. I was embarrassed, but it wasn't until I got home that my daughter told me I had these blotches all over my face. They went away, but came back again today when I went out. I'm really a little frightened about it. I have an appointment to see the doctor this afternoon."

We looked at her carefully. Her cheeks and her forehead were dull red. So were the backs of her hands. I said, "You know, it looks as if it's hit you everywhere that you were exposed."

"It's a crazy question," my wife asked, "but are you allergic to the cold?"

Hazel looked at us in bewilderment. "I never have been, but what else could it be?"

Her doctor agreed. She was allergic to cold, windy weather, but fortunately there was a very simple solution.

"I simply stay indoors when a cold wind is blowing," she told us a few days later when the blotches had faded. "If I must go out I cover all parts of me that are exposed. I wear gloves and a scarf and—oh yes—my new face mask."

Dos and Don'ts

Emphysema patients should make every effort to live in an unpolluted area with low humidity. They should avoid cities and low-lying places. Usually the trauma of a move is a serious factor to consider in deciding to relocate, but since emphysema is such a deadly disease, the risk of that trauma should be taken.

If you suffer from asthma, bronchitis, or any other lung diseases, be wary of exercise. Jogging in foggy or hazy weather can make things worse. Take extra precautions on foggy days. Stay inside and avoid exertion.

Keep a close watch on how you react during thunderstorms.

Some people are affected by the ionization of the air. If you are, this is a time to baby yourself. Put no extra strain on your lungs.

Fog can be a danger to some people suffering from respiratory disease. A cold, thick fog with trapped pollutants can be a killer. Stay at home and if you feel an asthmatic attack coming, consult your doctor.

If you are allergic and can't pinpoint what you are allergic to, try to match your attacks with weather and weather changes. Ignore friends who tell you you have a "psychosomatic" reaction. Search for a weather-connected cause.

If you are allergic to pollen, plan to get away to a pollen-free area during the worst part of the season. Keep a check on the weather and listen to newscasts that give the pollen count. Limit your activity on high-count days. Stay in an air-conditioned room and be sure your conditioner can filter out pollen.

All allergy sufferers should keep a chart comparing the weather—particularly humidity, fronts, and pressure—with their attacks. Keep track of the days when you are allergy-free, and note the weather on those days. It is just as important to know the weather that is good for you as it is to know the weather that makes you miserable.

Chapter Fifteen

Infections, Colds, Drugs, and Doctors

"I'm not a firm believer in the germ theory," Ronnie told me.

I said, "Nonsense! Next you'll be telling me the world is flat. The germ theory is a fact, not a theory."

"All the same, I don't believe in infections. Let me tell you, I've been exposed and nothing happened. I work in a hospital as an orderly and I've been around everything from diphtheria to the common cold, and I've come away as healthy as I am now!"

I looked at Ronnie's husky, solid build and nodded. "You must have natural resistance."

"That's not true either. There were times when I was out alone, hiking for a few days or off on the road, times when I haven't been in contact with anyone, and still I'll pick something up—a bad strep infection, a cold. Where is my natural resistance then?"

"If not the germ theory, then what?"

I won't go into Ronnie's wild answer. But I did believe his experience. It's not that uncommon. Some people get infectious diseases for no logical reason, it seems. Like Ronnie, they may be exposed to infection and resist it, or they may come down with an illness when there is no apparent exposure.

However, I don't throw out the germ theory any more than I dismiss the idea of natural resistance. Some diseases are caused by microorganisms, but whether we succumb or not is determined by the body's resistance.

Ronnie is a strong young man and apparently capable of resisting illness. Why did he come down with infections at certain times and resist them at others? He claimed his health was no different from one time to the other.

After reading the work of a German scientist with an Italian name, Dr. A. Marchionini, I found out that resistance can be a subtler and more complex process than I thought, and can depend on other factors besides body condition and exposure to infection.

Marchionini studied the acid-alkaline condition of the skin back in the 1930s and published papers that were ahead of their time. His work was rediscovered in the 1960s, and many cosmetic companies gave his acid-alkaline findings a catchy name. We began to hear of the *acid mantle* of the skin.

The skin, Marchionini declared, has a faintly acid coating, and this coating is a defense against harmful bacteria. They can't get a foothold on the skin while it remains acid, but let it go over to the alkaline side and we can pick up anything from impetigo and acne to a serious infection. Even a viral infection, such as the common cold or influenza, is repelled by that acid mantle.

What has all this to do with the weather? Quite a bit. You see, the acid mantle of the body forms when we sweat. Sweat evaporates in a cooling wind and leaves a faintly acid deposit.

If sweat does not evaporate, if it's caught in skin folds and stays there, it is attacked by bacteria that always live on the skin and is broken down into alkaline substances. Not only does this give us a rather rich odor, but it also leaves a pathway for infection.

This means that any weather condition—temperature, humidity, air movement—that affects the rate at which we sweat and the evaporation of that sweat can influence the growth of harmful microorganisms on the skin—and their entry into the body.

There you have it. If you dress too warmly in cold weather, if you wear clothes that do not let moisture escape, you'll sweat uncomfortably and the sweat won't dry and leave behind protective acid. That nice acid condition of your skin will change to alkaline, and you'll be open to infection.

This is only one possible pathway through which weather affects body resistance. Another pathway is more direct. Our nose, upper throat, the passage to our lungs, and our lungs themselves are all lined with a membrane of cells that keeps them moist by secreting mucus. In normal amounts, this mucus is a useful lubricant. Too little of it can dry us out; too much can cause anything from a runny nose to death by choking.

If the lining of the nose and throat dry out, then tiny splits, tears, or fissures appear in the membranes, and these are perfect lodging places for viruses or bacteria. A hot, dry wind or an overheated room will dry out the nose's membranes. So will a cold frosty day or a dry cold wind. (Studies have shown that an excess of positive ions will also dry out the membranes.)

Too much cold air causes the surface blood capillaries in the nasal passages to constrict. Less blood flows through them, and this is another reason why the lining may dry out and crack. A normal amount of humidity allows the breathing system to stay moist and healthy. Too much humidity makes it difficult to breathe. It creates excess mucus, which blocks the oxygen from the tissue.

Does Weather Cause Colds?

Another fact that seems to give the edge to weather as a dominant cause of colds is their synchronization pattern. If you chart all the cases of colds throughout the United States, you'll find that there are ups and downs according to each month. The incidence is up in October, down a bit in December, up again in January.

The same up-and-down pattern is true for Europe, and it seems to indicate that the weather in those months is more important than the contact factor. You catch a cold from someone, but only at certain times of the year. The weather in some way—and there are many ways it can happen—affects the body's heat-regulating mechanism, the hypothalamus, even the acid mantle, and we are open to attack. Our defenses are down.

The weather pattern that is most likely to cause flurries of colds is the passage of cold fronts, or the high barometric pressure that typically follows such fronts. A series of cold fronts, one after the other, brings even more colds with it.

Dr. F. Sargent, an American physician, matched weather patterns with the colds of students at Exeter Academy in New Hampshire. He examined 2,000 of them aged fourteen to nineteen years, and found that, indeed, when cold fronts passed they came down with more colds. But he also found the curious fact that certain types of schoolboys had most of their colds at different times of the year.

To begin with, Dr. Sargent divided the boys into three types based on height and weight. Type 1 were tall and slender; Type 2 were short and broad; Type 3 he called normal. In autumn and winter most of the colds were caught by the Type 1's—the tall, slender boys. In the spring most of the cold victims were the Type 2's—the short, broad boys. The Type 3's, the normals, caught colds indiscriminately.

All this hints at another aspect of weather sensitivity. It

may well be that physical stature determines how weather sensitive we are. Further studies should be made, and Types 1, 2, and 3 should be matched against symptoms, diseases, and weather patterns.

I have questioned nearly a hundred adults, each of whom fell into one of the three types, and my findings agree with Dr. Sargent's results. I found, too, that the Type 1's tend to be more weather sensitive than the Types 2's, but so small a sample permits no definitive conclusions.

How Weather Affects Infections

A number of other factors, all influenced by the weather, affect susceptibility to colds and other diseases. Gamma globulin is one. This substance in the blood gives us an immunity against many diseases. It also reacts to weather. When the weather changes, our supply of gamma globulin changes. Cold or warm air masses moving in can cause the change; so can seasonal differences.

Gamma globulin, the defense against infections, fluctuates with weather fronts. So does the level of certain hormones connected with resistance to disease.

The stress of a sudden cold or hot spell affects the hypothalamus, another control unit in the defense system. Hundreds of researchers have published papers detailing experiment after experiment to investigate how the weather affects our defense systems in the struggle against disease, but it is difficult to conduct a controlled research on human beings. Outside of prisons, where boredom helps in recruiting volunteers, few people will agree to have their lives so considerably disrupted.

Mice are more amenable. We can do what we want with them and even the ASPCA won't object. Dr. H. Colvin, at the Laboratory for Experimental Medicine in Cincinnati, took two groups of healthy laboratory mice and spent three weeks slowly adapting them to different temperatures. He kept the relative humidity constant at 60 percent, but one group of mice was adapted to 91° in one room, and the other to 65° in another room.

The second step was to inoculate each group with various disease bacteria to see how they survived. The mice in the warm room lived longer than those in the cold, but they couldn't resist infections as well. It took four times as many bacteria to kill the cold-room mice as it did the warm. Dr. Colvin concluded that the reason was probably the fact that the warm-room mice lived more slowly because of the heat. They had a lower metabolism and a lower energy level. The cold-room mice burned up their fuel more quickly. They could fight off the germs better, but their lives were short and cold. Perhaps they burned themselves out.

This animal work was applied to men. Another researcher, Dr. A. Locke of Pittsburgh, checked the metabolism of a group of men and compared it with their resistance to cold. Those who resisted cold best had the highest metabolism. He obviously couldn't say anything about their life span.

With heat indicated as a possible factor in increasing our susceptibility to serious infections, Dr. C. A. Mills of Cincinnati checked the records for acute appendicitis in twenty-five American cities. He found that the disease hit twice as often during summer heat waves as it did during the winter. Complications from appendicitis also were more frequent in the summer. Summer is no time to get either an infection of any kind or an infectious disease.

The weather affects us and our defense system, and, in so doing, affects the course of the disease itself. But weather has an even more direct effect on infectious diseases. Air currents can and do carry bacteria and viruses. In England, some time ago, a group of researchers were asked to do some studies for the air-hygiene committee of London's Medical Research

Council. A number of schools were having serious epidemics of measles and colds. What was causing them?

Researchers took air samples from each school and conducted tests to see which classroom had the highest number of bacteria. They were able to pinpoint the offending classrooms, and also lay the blame on certain wind currents. But one teacher, looking at the results, noted a curious relationship. The classrooms with the most impurities were also the rooms with the most talkative students.

Loose talk spreads germs was the conclusion, but there had to be a breeze around to pick up the germs.

Once the germs are in the air and drifting around, other weather factors can influence them. Certain bacteria will become airborne in the form of spores and then high humidity will start them developing and multiplying.

Another way for weather to influence the spread of disease is through the intervention of insects. Insects are much affected by weather, and therefore when they spread disease the weather is affecting us indirectly. This is far too complex a subject to more than mention, but the mosquito, of all the insects we encounter, is undoubtedly the most troublesome. In other lands, and in some parts of the United States, it is a deadly carrier of malaria. A few facts about the mosquito are worth knowing.

The malarial mosquito is attracted to different people by differences in smell. Babies are bitten more than grown-ups, and males more than females. The smell, entomologists decided, was due to sweat and the acids it contains, which takes us right back to weather. The greater the heat, the more we sweat, and the more we sweat, the more mosquitoes are attracted to us, and the greater our chances of malaria, yellow fever, and dengue fever—a disease endemic to certain islands of the West Indies.

The common cold, all the evidence seems to indicate, occurs most frequently in February and March and least frequently in September. Falling temperatures and rising humidity go along with the greatest number of colds. Other infectious diseases studied by biometeorologists also seem to be closely linked to weather patterns. There are more cases of tonsillitis after a cold front passes over. Influenza is at its height in December and February, but there are cases all year round. The great epidemic of 1918 occurred during dry, cold weather.

Meningitis peaks in February and March. Streptococcal infections seem to be at their highest during periods of low humidity. Scarlet fever, also caused by a strep bacterium, peaks in the cold months—February and March in New York and Chicago. In general this is a disease of the cold season. There are three times as many cases in the North as in the South.

Sinusitis has traditionally been related to the weather, and there are people who claim that differences in climate bring on sinus attacks. "In New York, I'm fine," one friend told me, "but let me go to Chicago and it's murder. I can feel my sinuses fill up."

I asked a well-known otolaryngologist, Dr. Decio Escobar of Waterbury, Connecticut, about this. "I can't begin to list the number of so-called cases of sinusitis I have treated," Dr. Escobar told me, "and of course, I do see a connection with the weather, but—and it's a big but—usually what is called sinusitis by the patient isn't that at all."

"What is it?" I asked.

"Sinusitis is a misnomer. What they are actually talking about is an allergic reaction of the nose and sinuses. You know the lining of the nose and the sinuses is the same; both react to the same allergens—and of course the reaction seems to be related to weather."

"Why do you say that it 'seems to be'?"

"Because it isn't the weather itself that causes the problem; it's things related to weather. In the spring it's pollen, in the summer it's grasses, and in the fall weeds."

"And humidity and air pressure?" I asked.

He shook his head. "I've never been able to find any relationship, even when sinusitis is confirmed by radiological diagnosis."

Do Cold Fronts Trigger Glaucoma?

The first man to connect the weather with eye problems was Dr. K. Steindorff, in turn-of-the-century Berlin. Dr. Steindorff may have been old-fashioned as he drove through the cobbled streets to the ophthalmic clinic, but he was far-sighted enough to notice an odd pattern in the number of patients admitted to the clinic for attacks of glaucoma, the disease that causes a build-up of pressure within the eyeball and leads to blindness if not treated.

Dr. Steindorff saw cases of glaucoma all year round, but in the winter there seemed more than usual. He checked his records carefully and found that more than one-quarter of the cases occurred in January, the coldest month of the year in Berlin. All the worst attacks, he found, happened on very cold days, just as the summer attacks took place on very hot days.

"Changes in blood pressure due to extreme temperature conditions are very possible in older people who suffer from advanced arteriosclerosis," he wrote in a paper, which he sent off to a prestigious medical journal and which served as an inspiration for other ophthalmologists.

A few years later a survey at the ophthalmic clinic of Tübingen found the same fact—cold weather brought on most of the cases of glaucoma. At the same time, another study from Calcutta, where cold isn't much of a problem, found that most cases occurred during the monsoon when the rainfall and sunless days seem to go on forever. In Italy, during the first decade of this century, the findings were reconfirmed, as they were in the next decade at the ophthalmic clinic in Basel.

In the 1930s, a study from Japan found that sunny, pleasant areas reported very little glaucoma compared to the rest of the nation. In fact, the incidence of glaucoma was very low altogether in Japan and in China too, where the average blood pressure was lower than it was in the West.

Since glaucoma is a disease in which the internal pressure of the eye increases, it seemed logical that barometric highs and lows should affect it. And so, in the 1930s, Dr. H. Fischer at the ophthalmic clinic in Leipzig matched glaucoma attacks against weather, searching for a link with barometric pressure. He found no connection between barometric fluctuations and attacks, but he did find that 88 percent of the attacks of glaucoma occurred when either cold or warm fronts passed over.

Another study from the ophthalmic clinic of Basel confirmed Fischer's observation that a majority of cases occurred when fronts passed. Again in the 1940s and in the 1950s, with more accurate statistical methods, 80 percent of the cases of glaucoma were linked to cold air masses, and this time they also implicated air turbulence.

A final study in 1958 found that acute attacks occurred "just before and during unpleasant weather changes."

Our growing understanding of the connection between cold fronts and glaucoma, starting with Dr. Steindorff and coming to maturity in the sophisticated methods of the 1950s, was made possible by the close cooperation of large ophthalmic clinics with physicians and scientists interested in biometeorology. The records were all available, and researchers were able to determine the exact onset of a glaucoma attack and match it against the weather of the moment.

The inevitable conclusion was that acute glaucoma is *meteorotropic*; the attacks are related to the weather. The disease is influenced by (and dependent on) weather changes, specifically on air turbulence caused by the passage of cold fronts.

This conclusion gives us clues to the cause of glaucoma. Other studies carried out on blood pressure and weather turned up the fact that in winter, in the coldest months of the year, when cold fronts are most frequent, the blood pressure rises. This occurs in healthy people and even more so in people with arteriosclerotic disease. In the Netherlands the death rate from arterial disease parallels the incidence of acute attacks of glaucoma, and when the two are compared in other countries the same parallel will probably show up. Since the heat-regulation system of the body, the hypothalamus, is also linked to the movement of cold fronts, in studies of that organ and of arteriosclerosis we shall undoubtedly find a clue to what causes glaucoma.

When Doctors Disagree

Eventually, when biometeorology is accepted in our country as fully as it has been in Europe, we may be able to uncover similar links between other diseases and weather changes, along with clues to their management. Cancer, heart disease, arthritis, lung disease, allergies, and infectious diseases seem to be connected to weather. How many other illnesses are linked as well, and how closely?

The main stumbling block to research in this country has been a tendency on the part of physicians to dismiss the importance of weather when they think about it at all. Very few seem to have made the connection. Rheumatologists are aware of it, but most of those to whom I spoke asked, "What's the point? What can we do?" It was only when I pressed them that they admitted that the *patient* could do something.

Cardiologists seem only dimly aware of the connection. I spoke to a noted New York City specialist who had just treated a close friend of mine. "He's a wonderful doctor," my friend said, "a doctor's doctor. Talk to him. He should know about the connection between weather and the heart if anyone does."

My interview was disappointing. "All I can tell you," he said, "is that my patients with bone repair, those who have had their chests opened for heart surgery, feel pain in the healed bones whenever there's any change in the weather."

I had heard about bone pain; it is one of the most common symptoms of weather sensitivity. If a bone is damaged in any way, no matter how well it heals, the chances of its becoming a weather indicator are great. The same is true for amputations. Many people feel severe pain in missing limbs when the weather changes. It is phantom pain: The spot that hurts is gone, but the pain is real. It must have something to do with the nerves that have been cut when the amputation took place. The remainder of the nerves still react to the weather and send the sensation of pain in the missing limb to the brain.

The cardiologist could cite examples of bone pain, but when I told him of more down-to-earth effects—changes in sedimentation rates when the weather changes, changes in cholesterol levels, blood pressure and coagulation—he shook his head.

"I've never heard of those studies. How controlled are they? How accurate? I'd have to see the data. I'd have to see it compared . . ." And so it went.

He was right, of course. You cannot accept studies unless you have confidence in their validity. But all the studies I mentioned and described in this book are reputable. They have all been published in sound journals, and they are all available in medical libraries. In most cases, American physicians are simply ignorant of, or not interested in, the effects of weather on their patients, except as a medical curiosity.

Nor is their attitude wholly without reason. A German cardiologist and biometeorologist who asked me not to use his name ("it would only get me into trouble with my colleagues") put the case very clearly.

"Fifty years ago, even thirty years ago, it would have been of enormous help to cardiologists to know what effect weather had on, for example, the coagulation of the patient's blood. They could have geared a great deal of their therapy to the weather. But today it's no help to us in treating our patients.

We have such excellent anticoagulants, we can control our patients' blood with an exactness that weather therapy would never permit. We can't take risks with anything as wayward as the weather; we want the certainty of drugs. But don't quote me. My fellow biometeorologists would feel I was selling them out."

"But if that's so, why are you so intrigued with biometeorology?"

"Scientific curiosity. It's a fascinating field and wide open. You don't need a laboratory. Any scientist who can get his hands on patients' records, interview people, and read the daily weather reports can play the biometeorological research game. I love it."

"You say it might not help the physician in treating his patient," I said, "but you haven't said anything about the patients themselves. Surely it's of value to them to know what effect the weather has on them, so they can avoid certain climates and weather patterns, plan their vacations around times of the year when their condition will not be upset, even know what is upsetting them and how serious or trivial it is. That's a great deal of help."

"Ah, but that's a whole different story. We physicians are not concerned with that. We want to help our patients and we have all we can do to keep up with the new drugs. To add the weather to it would complicate our lives unnecessarily."

That still did not convince me, and a well-known ophthalmologist increased my dissatisfaction. He was more concerned with biometeorology than his colleagues. "It's something I always bear in mind," he told me one evening in a Manhattan bar. "Look, I do a great many operations for cataracts. I was at the ophthalmic clinic of Dresden University after the Allies had fire-bombed that city. What a mess. It was in the fifties and they had records that showed that there were more hemorrhages in the anterior chamber of the eye from January to May.

"You get a lot of active cold fronts passing over Dresden

then, cold polar air. One man there suggested that the hemorrhages might be due to an increase of the pressure inside the eye after an operation. This wouldn't affect firm, healthy tissue, but it could blow out the newly developed scar of a cataract adhesion. Cold fronts and air turbulence cause low barometric pressure, which would cause the eyeball to expand.

"Hell, it's only one man's theory, but you can be damned sure I take that kind of weather change into account, and I try to schedule my cataract operations for the time of year when there are no active fronts passing. I try to. If it's not emergency surgery I usually can do it. It may not help, but it doesn't hurt."

How Weather Affects Your Reactions to Drugs

It is not only the effect of the weather on the patient and on the patient's condition that should concern physicians, but also the effect of the weather on drugs. Many pharmacologists have pointed out that the same drug may act differently under different weather conditions. Understandably, this is not something that drug houses publicize. They would of course prefer that a given dosage of a drug work the same way at all times, but this simply is not the case.

Take digitalis, a powerful drug that helps to regulate the heart rate. A group of pharmacologists at the Pharmacological Research Laboratory in Baltimore noticed that a solution of digitalis becomes more toxic when the barometer is falling. This means that a patient taking digitalis should decrease the dose when a storm threatens.

The same results with digitalis were found when the drug was tested at high altitudes. And, of course, the air pressure decreases the higher one goes. That is, the barometer falls just as it does when a thunderstorm breaks, but the movements during a thunderstorm are not as great as those that occur as one ascends from lowland to mountain.

This did not happen only once. The experimenter repeated the test on and off for seven years, and each time he found the same results. Others duplicated his results. One researcher, in fact, divided a batch of digitalis into two parts. Half he left in San Francisco at sea level to be tested by an assistant. They synchronized their watches and then, with the other half, he drove up to the Tioga Pass in the Sierra Nevada Mountains. There, at 9,000 feet above sea level, he tested the digitalis while his assistant tested it down in the city. The drug was administered to 144 different pigeons in 288 trials. The mountain batch was more than twice as strong as the same batch down in the city!

I asked a number of cardiologists if they would prescribe different doses of digitalis before thunderstorms, and they all looked at me as if I were insane. Yet this research is not new; it's been around for forty years.

Digitalis is not the only drug affected by the weather. Morphine, too, becomes more toxic when cold fronts pass over. It is least active when the weather is stable.

The stress of cold weather also changes the way we react to a drug. Furthermore, cold can change the action of some antibiotics (and sunlight can make other antibiotics deadly), of insulin, and of some vitamins.

"Exposure to cold," Dr. S. Rheiman wrote, after completing a study under a grant from the U.S. Public Health Service, "can induce marked changes in the absorption and the physiologic or the toxic effects of a large number of drugs. The absorption of a specific drug can be either increased of inhibited."

Dos and Don'ts

The most serious weather factor affecting the common cold is the passage of a cold front. When one passes, your chances of catching a cold increase. If you are tall and skinny, your

chances of coming down with a cold are even greater, especially
in the autumn or winter. Short, broad people are more likely to
catch cold in the spring. People with average builds seem to
get them any time a cold front passes.

But remember, these are all "chances." Not everyone catches
cold with every cold front. Good health, plenty of sleep, and a
sound diet can do more to prevent colds than any amount of
fine weather.

Tonsillitis seems to follow the same pattern: People who
are prone to the infection pick it up more readily when a cold
front passes.

A final word on colds: They are more prevalent when the
temperature falls and the humidity rises.

Cold fronts are also potentially dangerous to glaucoma
patients. If you have glaucoma, stay indoors at such times and
avoid exertion. You might also, if you have any say in the
matter, try not to have surgery for glaucoma when a cold
front is predicted.

If you have recently undergone any kind of surgery, expect
your scar to ache when the humidity is high and the air pressure
is low.

If you are taking a prescription drug, ask your doctor
whether changes in the weather can affect the action of the
drug, or your reaction to it. He may have to do a little research
on this question, but it will be worth it to you and his other
patients.

Chapter Sixteen

How Weather Affects Your Sex Life

I had asked a number of obstetricians if they were aware of any connection between births and the weather, and one night I received a call from one of them. It was after eleven, and I was a bit startled, but he reassured me. "I've just delivered a whopper of a baby, over ten pounds. It suddenly occurred to me, here it is the end of June, and I swear, five out of every six babies are eight pounds or over. I've never seen such a healthy, round-faced bunch."

I met him the next day for coffee, and I asked, "Were you kidding last night? Do you really get bigger babies in the summer?"

"I was serious," he said, "and afterwards I had to hang around the hospital, waiting for one of my ladies to make up her mind about delivery. So I stepped into the library and dug into the *Index Medicus*—way back. I found something interesting, something that confirms what I told you. Some studies done over fifty years ago found that the biggest babies were born in June or July, the smallest from December to March. The weight difference was even more exaggerated if you didn't count the firstborn baby, just the later ones in a family."

"And today?" I asked.

"A lot of parents stop at one, but in those days they had big families. You know, there were other researchers who found the same thing—bigger babies born in the summer. And they weren't casual observers like me. One examined the birth weights of over twelve thousand babies, and another twenty-five thousand—that's a lot of babies!"

"Did they find what caused it?"

He shrugged. "I guess it was the same thing that causes it now. They felt it was the increase in sunlight."

"But why should that make bigger babies?"

He rubbed his head. "It's a complicated business. It could be nutrition—mothers eat more protein in the winter while the baby is developing. But I'm inclined to think it's hormonal. The extra sunlight gives more stimulation to the optic nerve and that affects the hypothalamus and hormonal secretions. The pituitary gland is affected too. These hormonal alterations could easily affect the baby's growth. Remember, this is a statistical thing. Not all babies are bigger, but a significant number are.

"Incidentally, there were a few other interesting weather-linked facts that I found in the old books. Do you know about the moon?"

"You mean more babies being born during the full moon."

Disappointed, he said, "I thought I'd surprise you with that. But let's look at births. Do you know that there are more babies born in January? Which means that there are more babies conceived in April? What is there about the spring that stimulates sex?"

I couldn't answer that question, but I knew that, whatever the reason, there was something unusual about spring conceptions.

Clarence Mills, the granddaddy of biometeorology, wrote a fascinating book about it back in the 1920s. He went through *Who's Who* and found that an unusually large number of the people listed in it were conceived in April, May, and June. He said it indicated that children conceived in the spring tended to be smarter, or at least more successful than the rest of us. Other studies, however, suggest that these spring conceptions run a risk of summer heat in the third month, which can cause possible birth defects, and not such smart children.

My obstetrician friend told me of still another conception fact that intrigued him.

"Did you know that a lot of extra babies were conceived during New York's electrical blackout? We obstetricians were kept busy nine months later."

"What else was there to do in the dark?" I asked, and then, as a thought hit me, I said, "Is it at all possible, or is it too far out, to suggest that cutting all that electric current freed some sexual inhibitions?"

He looked at me strangely. "You know I had never thought of that, but electricity seems to have an effect on birth, if not on conception. A guy named Reiter in Bavaria in 1950 checked electromagnetic long waves . . ."

"Sferics?"

"That's a new word to me. But he checked the long waves after thunderstorms and matched them against births. There were eight percent more babies born on days with a considerable disturbance of those electromagnetic waves. How about that?"

I made a note of it and said, "You've been a lot of help."

"Good. But I've thought of something else to go with the birth-date business. When my ladies are ready to have a baby, if it's a planned event, I suggest that they arrange things so that the baby is born in the early spring."

"Why is that?"

"Well, then the baby has comfortable warm weather for

those early months. By the time the cold of winter comes, the baby is old enough to handle it. Also, they can be outdoors a lot in those early months."

"You think that fresh air is that important?"

"Yes. I like to see a new baby play with only a diaper on. I like my mothers to get their babies outside right away. I hate having a baby spend those early months in a dry, overheated apartment."

"Careful. You're encroaching on the pediatrician's turf."

"Maybe. But I still say good weather in the first three months makes a healthier baby."

I pondered my friend's words for a long time, then decided to do some research on my own. If the weather has an effect on birth weights and birth dates, could it also have an effect on any other elements of reproduction or sex?

How Weather Affects Conception

When I started my research I thought of sex in terms of the sexual act. To my surprise I found an unusual connection between weather and the sex of the baby—even a possible method of increasing your chances of having a boy or a girl. Conceive your child during very cold or very hot weather, and the chances of having a boy increase. Conceive during warm weather, and the chances of having a girl increase—at least, that's what a Chicago statistical study indicates. Of course, this doesn't mean that all babies conceived in a December cold snap will be boys. It does mean that significantly over half will.

The reason, according to Dr. W. F. Petersen, who reported the fact, probably is the condition of the mother. Her metabolism would be higher in very cold weather, and this would affect the metabolism of her egg cells. In some way, this increased metabolism of the egg at fertilization and during early growth might "incline the egg towards maleness."

The explanation seems foolish to me, since sex is determined by the chromosomes in the sperm. Other studies are necessary to confirm Petersen's results before we adopt weather eugenics.

Another group of researchers found another weather-sex connection. As a rule, more boys are born than girls, and more boy babies die early in the first months. This is nature's way of equalizing the boy-girl balance. By the time both are eighteen and ready to match up with each other, there is an approximate one-to-one ratio—provided no wars have intervened.

But during the summer months the ratio shifts. Fewer boys born in the summer die during the first months. There seems no reason for this unless some weather factor is responsible for the winter deaths.

As far as fertility goes, light seems to affect sexual desire. The pathways are very devious and include the pituitary gland, the central nervous system, and possibly the pineal gland (our atrophied "third eye"). What light does to libido is still uncertain. A study of births in England showed that over an eight-year period the greatest number of conceptions occurred during the days with most light, but who knows if it was light or fine Jone weather that encouraged conception? Certainly the babies born after the New York City blackout indicate stimulation by the dark.

Psychological tests have been done on men and women, strangers to one another, who were put together in a darkened room. Within a half hour they were hugging and kissing each other! Could this have been the masking effect of the dark? They knew they would never see one another again, and there was no responsibility, no commitment.

Lovemaking, however, does seem to be affected by light. A friend of mine told me that light had a profound influence on his libido.

"I've made love in some very far-out places, and it was always an impulsive thing. I remember waking up with a woman in a summer house with a huge glass wall looking out on a deserted beach. The sun was up, but low in the sky and flooding the room with light, so much light that I could hardly open my eyes. I suddenly felt an incredible rush of sexual energy. I woke my partner up, and she had the same reaction. It was heavenly."

Another friend, a woman in her early twenties, told me she was aroused by thunderstorms. "I'm frightened of them in a way, but at the same time they set my whole body tingling. I'm a pushover for any man I'm with, so much so that when I know a storm is coming I try to be by myself, unless I really like the guy."

"Just thunderstorms?" I asked, thinking of sferics.

"That's it. But it's funny. When I was younger I was out with a boyfriend in his car, and he drove out to a deserted spot near the river, right below the big hydroelectric plant that serves the whole county. He said it was a lovers' lane, though we were the only ones there, the only car parked. I had been lukewarm towards him, but the moment he parked the car, I went into my tingling act. I couldn't resist him." She grinned. "Actually, he couldn't resist me."

A hydroelectric plant and atmospheric electricity could both produce long electromagnetic waves—sferics. But are there any scientific indications that sferics have an effect on the libido? I asked a neurologist about this, and he shook his head. "You're in a very tricky area. I've heard of sferics producing an excess of thyroid, and it is possible that this is an answer. Too much thyroid excites you in every way. It speeds up your metabolism, and if the right amount is released, it could stimulate your libido.

"But you must remember you are in a psychological area here. I think it much more likely that your friend was stimulated mentally by the storm and reacted to that."

"And the hydroelectric station?"

He smiled. "We really don't know what sferics can do, but tell her to stay away from power plants."

How Your Responses Change with the Weather

To try to find out some more about the weather's effect on sexual activity, I questioned men and women in three age groups: from sixteen to thirty, from thirty to fifty, and from fifty upward. Their answers were revealing.

Lorraine, a thirty-five-year-old single businesswoman, told me, "There is no doubt about it. Whenever a young man's fancy turns to spring, mine is not far behind. The first warm weather of June, and vibes go out. I respond like mad. The whole world seems to come alive, and so does my sexual self. I'm ready to fall in love, and I always do. I take chances in the spring, emotional chances, and I never regret them, at least not until summer comes!"

Larry, twenty and a college senior, said, "With me it's not seasonal; it depends on what kind of day it is. Give me a hot, humid day and I couldn't care less about sex. You could put me into bed with Farrah Fawcett-Majors and I'd just yawn. But a cold, crisp winter day with a clear sky, watch out! I could take on all the women in the freshman class." He added, "And another thing, on a cold night if I get into bed with a girl I may feel chilly to start with, but after a few minutes of lovemaking I'm ready to throw off all the blankets. My skin heats up and I can feel my blood rising, and certainly my heart beats faster."

This warmth that Larry felt once he started making love is a common sexual experience. The sexual act and its preliminaries start the blood flowing faster, and the blood vessels near the surface dilate. Our blood flows through them more easily, warming the skin.

Elton, sixty-two and married, a grandfather looking forward to his first great-grandchild, said, "Weather related? I think it's more a case of what time of day. Sex at night is difficult. My wife and I are both too tired, and there's too much hustle in the morning. I don't feel sexual at either of those times.

My most sexual period is early afternoon. I'm rested and somehow, I don't know, I just feel more alert then, more alive."

Lisa, who is twenty-four and divorced, said, "You won't believe this, but a full moon does the trick for me, and sometimes it does me in. Now I'm a Sagittarius, and that may be the reason, or maybe it's the fact that the guys that I go with are usually Aries. Anyway, I have an off-again, on-again romance with a guy I just don't like. He's an Aries, too. I'll break it off, and then if I'm not with someone else when the moon is full, I find that I call him. I don't know why. I always do—and I'm always hurt."

Jerry, thirty-one, married, and always on the road, said, "My work keeps me away from my family. I like the traveling thing, and the only problem is sex. It's not really a problem, because I can get as much as I want. The guilt is the problem, but that doesn't stop me. The point is, let the weather be lousy, raining, and miserable or muggy and the guilt wins out. I sit in my motel and watch TV. But let the weather be great—you know, one of those classy sunny days—and I'm hot to trot with anyone."

Leah, fifty-five, is widowed, but leads a very active social life. "I don't stay home and brood. I get out and I go, and if I meet a nice man, OK, I'm not a prude, and I still have a figure. I'm not ashamed to get into a bathing suit. But conditions have to be right." Pressed about conditions, she said a little awkwardly, "I can't stand making love in hot weather. The spring is my time, or a nice clear day. I like the rain, too. There's something about cuddling up with a sympathetic friend when the rain is beating against the windowpanes."

These people are typical of those I interviewed. I changed their names but not their feelings about the weather. Sexually, some were weather sensitive. Some reacted negatively to humidity; it turned them off. Others felt a lack of sexual stimulation in very cold weather. But four out of six responded to clear, cold weather or to the softness of a spring day. They spoke a very definite sexual weather language.

That ratio—four out of six—held pretty firm for most of the weather-sensitive people I talked to. Some said weather didn't matter. They saw no connection between their sexuality and rain, shine, humidity, or whatnot. A few said any time, any place, any kind of weather.

So there's nothing exceptional about responding sexually to fine weather. The poets always sang of spring and matched clear skies to unclouded eyes, and in nature spring is the traditional mating time. But the birds and the bees and all the wild animals mate in the spring for the same reason my obstetrician friend advised his mothers to have their babies in the spring. Most animals have shorter gestation periods than humans. A bird or a mammal needs fair weather to raise a family because by the end of the summer the young must be ready to weather the winter.

Have humans carried over this law of nature from a more primitive time? The late Dr. Ellsworth Huntingdon of Yale tested a group of Yale college students in a number of simulated weather conditions and concluded that they were at their mental and physical peak when the weather was at its peak, an ideal 64° and a relative humidity below 80 percent. This of course is ideal spring weather, and ideal autumn weather too.

Research indicates that different kinds of weather have different effects on the sexual and reproductive systems. In all mammals, long periods of temperature above 90° may cause delayed puberty and irregularity in the length of the menstrual cycle. It may shorten the time they're in heat and result in smaller babies and distorted sperm.

In ideal weather there is an increased production of sex hormones and sperm in humans. With a general body pickup, the libido perks up, too, so there's a physiological reason why our fancies "lightly turn to thoughts of love."

If spring is the time for lovers, what about summer? Although many novelists have written about the eroticism of hot, sultry days and nights, the men and women I interviewed felt otherwise.

Kim is typical of most of the younger women. "The heat turns me off. Making love when your body is covered with sweat is just distasteful, and the bedclothes get all tangled. Yuch. I just feel no energy in real summer heat and no desire nohow."

Most of the men felt the same way, but a sizable number found the heat stimulating. "There's something about two sweaty bodies that turns me on," Keith, the same age as Kim, told me. "I like the odor of it. I feel it's like the running together of juices, and there's a lazy sexuality to lovemaking in the heat. Someday I'd like to try it out in the open under a really hot sun. Wow!"

A few women agreed, especially on odor. They felt there was something sexually attractive in the odor of a man's sweat. "Not stale sweat, but the sweat of a nice clean body."

Where the Best Sex Is

In discussing the results of my questionnaire with a psychologist, she pointed out that many women use heat as an excuse to avoid sex.

"But don't those women have sexual problems?"

"We all have sexual problems. Those are women who don't really understand that they dislike sex. They think they like it, but they invent logical-seeming excuses why they shouldn't have it, like the distasteful odor of sweat. In actual fact, sweat has erototropic volatile substances in it that attract the other sex."

"Then you feel that nature intended men and women to be sexy in the hot weather?"

"You mustn't talk of nature as if it's a reasoning being.

Nature did not intend; mankind evolved to its present condition. To set the record straight, there are just as many men who invent unconscious excuses to avoid sex—'I've had a hard day at the office. I'm exhausted. I have this awful headache'—and often the weather is behind the excuse."

"But what I hoped my questioning would discover was: Which is of prime importance? Emotions, libido, or weather? How much does the weather move us?"

"In my field it is the unconscious and the emotions. I can't answer your questions about people being sexier in hot weather. Some doctors say no."

As an example of one physician who didn't agree with her, my psychologist friend referred me to the work of Dr. Lawrence Jackman, director of the Human Sexuality Program at the Albert Einstein College of Medicine in New York City. He agrees with the high-heat–low-sex formula. He points out that the fantasy of better sex in a hot climate is usually just that, a fantasy, because under any extreme weather conditions all the body energies decline, and that includes the sex drive.

But some people who should know say people are more sexually aroused in hot weather. A travel agent in Chicago told me, "The young people I book for vacations to sunny hot places are all very sexually active. I get reports back from them and from the hotels I send them to. I don't know. It may be just getting away from their home and job. But it doesn't happen when I arrange a trip to a cold climate. I think it's the effect of the weather, especially in the tropics. Maybe it's those long siestas, or all those bikinis. Whatever it is, I know there's a lot more casual sex in tropical climates."

In search of some scientific support for either side of the question—does hot weather increase libido or decrease it?—I mentioned the subject to Dr. Ranscht-Froemsdorff in Freiburg. Dr. Froemsdorff had worked with sferics and ionization. "I found no effect of sferics on sexual desire," he told me. "But that hasn't been the direction of my research. I can say that the excess of positive ions such as you get with hot desert winds can turn off sexual activity, if only by causing headaches and irritability."

If positive ions turn sexual desire off, then a good case could be made for negative ions turning it on. These are supposed to put the entire body in a state of contentment and relaxation—surely a good way to enjoy sex. Negative ions are plentiful when the weather is springlike or crisp and cool.

Another possible answer came from a man I interviewed shortly after his honeymoon in New York. "We spent it in the Plaza Hotel, in one of those great suites overlooking Central Park, and it was the most wonderful time I ever had. We never got out of the room. We had all our meals sent up and we had a ball, and sex—my God," he said in an awed voice, "I never dreamed it could be so good."

I was amused at his enjoyment of the Plaza suite, and I put it all down to the honeymoon and getting away from everything for a while, until I saw an article in the *New York Post* which told of checking various places in the city with a portable ion meter that measures positive and negative ions.

The reporter found that the New York subway system had the heaviest load of positive ions. Nathan's Restaurant, a New York landmark, had a very high positive-ion count. So did the sixty-eighth floor of the World Trade Center, while F.A.O. Schwarz, the toy store, was not far behind.

Godiva, the very posh Fifth Avenue chocolate store, leaned towards the positive side, but strange to tell, the place that had the best ratio of negative to positive ions was "a $225-a-day suite at the Plaza, overlooking Central Park, with crystal chandeliers and marble fireplaces in both rooms." My honeymoon interviewee had more going for him than he realized.

(An aside: Don't count on sex in an air-conditioned room to overcome the oppressive heat of summer. Reports show that air conditioning takes the negative ions out of the air, and it may well be the negative ions that turn you on.)

One of the neurologists I talked to reminded me of the

findings I detailed earlier, that the brain has a regulator center that uses tiny amounts of electricity generated in the body. Any severe electrical storm can produce disturbances in brain-wave patterns and cause abnormal behavior.

"This can have a very serious effect on a person's sexual preference," the neurologist said.

"In what way?"

"It's not that measurable. The electricity can disturb us either way. It can send us up or down the sexuality scale. It can heighten performance, make us come alive and enjoy sexual encounters. It can make orgasm exceedingly intense— or it can send us down the scale, interfere with performance, and make it difficult to make love.

"On an emotional basis, the electric discharge of a storm, or even a coming storm, can make us irritable with our partner, quick to pick a fight, and reluctant to yield to suggestions. In fact, outside storms can lead to an inside one, a really stormy love affair."

It would be foolish on the basis of this to avoid a storm. Dr. Landsberg of the University of Maryland pointed out that we need the stress of different types of weather to function well, to stay mentally and physically alert. Weather stimulation keeps our bodies and minds in shape.

What it all adds up to: Indeed, the weather has a very strong hand in influencing sexual activity, but as one psychologist told me, "Our unconscious desires are still the dominant factor in making love and getting along with our lovers." You might paraphrase that in sexual weather language by saying, "Some like it hot, some like it cold—some like it any way, young or old!"

Chapter Seventeen

Diet and Weather

"Every day in every way I'm getting fatter and fatter," Al said sadly.

"What do you expect," his wife snapped at him, "on a diet of potatoes and bread? I can't get you to eat vegetables."

"In the army," Al said wistfully, "I ate the same way, as many potatoes as I wanted, and I never gained weight."

"Where were you stationed?" I asked.

"In the Aleutians."

"Maybe you were more active then."

He shook his head. "Not really. I spent all my time at a desk checking inventories in one of those damned quonset huts. Brother, was it cold!" He patted his ample belly. "I guess I'll just have to live with this."

I mentioned Al's hang-up with food to a psychologist. "Your friend's problem," he told me, "is too much civilization. With all its complexity, it's played hell with our simple instincts."

"What are our simple instincts in terms of food?" I asked.

"Like animals, we should eat to keep warm and stop eating to keep from getting too warm. It's as easy as that."

"I thought we ate because we were hungry?"

"Yes, but what makes us hungry? We civilized folks eat for taste, for social reasons, for status—the more expensive the food the better—and for neurotic reasons, to overcome insecurity, to satisfy the sucking needs, as a substitute for love and affection."

"But what about Al's army experience? Could he really eat as much as he wanted and still not gain weight?"

"Of course not. His memory is just a bit fuzzy. There was research done about that right after World War II when plenty of soldiers were still available for controlled experiments. Scientists studied the eating habits of a platoon of soldiers transferred to the far north, and they found, naturally enough, that as the temperature went down they ate more. They ate to keep warm. The important thing was: They didn't overeat. They ate more because in the arctic cold their bodies used up more food and they also dressed in heavier clothes and needed more energy to get about. But they only ate as much as they needed. They didn't, like your friend Al, eat themselves into obesity. Eating as much as you need, and then stopping, is a normal pattern of behavior."

I asked, "Does that mean it's better to diet in the winter than in the summer?"

"I'm not sure. But the same diet will certainly take off more weight in winter when you use more energy."

The best time to diet, a nutritionist told me, is in the early spring or in the fall. The winter is bad, and so is the summer, unless your diet is carefully planned by someone very familiar with the body's requirements.

I spoke to a public health nutritionist, Beverly Daniel, about this. Beverly, tall and slim, looks like an advertisement for good nutrition. I had heard her lecture at the New School for Social Research in New York and was impressed with her ideas.

"I've heard both that dieting in winter is good and that it's bad. Is it true that dieting in the winter helps?"

She nodded. "Of course. But all sorts of factors are involved. It's not only the *amount* you eat in cold weather that counts, but *what*. When healthy young men, like the soldiers you talk of, need more energy, given a free hand with food, or I should say a free mouth, instead of eating more they'll eat differently. For instance, a high-carbohydrate diet will give you more calories than a high-protein diet. And best of all is a high-fat diet. The Eskimos know that. Their diet is high in animal fat."

"Blubber and all that," I said.

"That's right."

"But I'm confused. Are you saying that eating fat is a good idea for dieting in winter?"

"You *are* confused! Eating fat is a good way to get fat. In very cold weather people need more energy. I'm saying that if you eat a diet heavy in carbohydrates—and by carbohydrates I mean fruit, vegetables, and whole-grain cereals—you get a better value in your energy-to-food ratio provided you get adequate protein as well. More energy will come from eating fat, sure, but I'm not talking about your city dweller. He really isn't that stressed by cold."

"And yet he does burn up more energy in the winter, right? And he uses more calories. Then if dieting in the winter makes sense, why do we eat lightly in the summer?"

She laughed. "We eat like that in the warm weather because it's more comfortable. Salads and cold soup and other summer foods contain more water, too, and we need more water in hot weather. But if you exercise in hot weather, then you need a well-balanced diet at that time, too."

"What about fat for the summer athlete?"

"Fat takes longer to digest. Carbohydrates digest faster and the athlete needs fast energy. But the interesting thing is that when we exercise like that, given a choice, we prefer carbohydrates to other foods. The same thing, incidentally, happens up in the mountains."

"You mean eating more carbohydrates?"

"Right. They tested soldiers stationed in mountain areas about three or four years ago, and found that they picked carbohydrates and sugars over fats and proteins when they had a chance. Up that high, fats are hard to digest."

"What about hot foods? I mean not temperature hot, but spicy. Why do people in the tropics favor very hot foods?"

"Well, the spicy foods cause you to break out in a sweat, and I guess the cooling effect of that is worth the pepper shock they go through. If you want some interesting ideas about the weather and food," Beverly added thoughtfully, when I was leaving, "I suggest you look over the work of Dr. Benjamin Frank."

A Diet to Resist the Cold

Following her advice, I found that Dr. Frank, a medical researcher, has written about resisting cold through diet. The reason some people are able to take the cold better than others, he believes, is that they have more nucleic acid in their diet. Nucleic acids are the stuff genetic dreams are made of. Every cell in our body has a full complement of chromosomes made up of nucleic acid.

Nucleic acid, Dr. Frank believes, is indirectly responsible for a human being's ability to withstand the cold. Like Charles Darwin before him, Dr. Frank is impressed with the ability of the Indians of Tierra del Fuego to weather intense cold. The reason, he believes, is their heavy diet of fish. Fish are very rich in nucleic acids, and this gives these Indians the ability to run around naked. (He is silent on the Australian aborigines, who also endure cold weather without clothes and who do not eat fish.)

Dr. Frank has experimented on himself with a diet heavy in nucleic acid, and he decided that it increased his cold tolerance. More to the point, he fed one group of laboratory mice a nucleic-acid-rich diet and another a normal diet and kept them both in a cold environment. The mice on the nucleic acid seemed more independent, or at least they slept apart. The other mice huddled together for warmth, according to Dr. Frank.

He put a number of his own patients on the diet and reported that they tolerated cold better.

The diet Dr. Frank offers to overcome the cold emphasizes nuts, beans, and fish—and lots of sardines. Is it fact or fad? I don't know anyone who has had positive results with the diet, but then I've only spoken to a few people who have tried it. Dr. Frank's diet has an impressive number of converts. What makes me dubious is that he also feels that the diet prevents aging. Unfortunately, the Tierra del Fuegans age rapidly. It's a tough life down there.

A physiologist who listened to me patiently when I discussed Dr. Frank's diet said, "Perhaps a fish-rich diet would help against the cold. And certainly Eskimos eat a lot of fish, but they also have a lot of fat in their diet. Fat and frequent meals are the best way of resisting severe cold, as far as I know."

"But why? Is there a reason behind that?"

"There is, especially when you get into experimental animal studies. A team of Japanese scientists from the Hokkaido University School of Medicine compared rats fed on a standard diet, where fourteen percent of their calories came from fat, with a group on a high-fat diet, where eighty percent of their calories came from fat. The rats on the high-fat diet were less sensitive to cold, particularly the older rats. The Japanese put it down to an influence on the thyroid."

"Then you think we should eat more fats in cold weather."

"Hold on. You're jumping to conclusions. If you want to resist cold stress, if you want to keep from losing weight and be physically active in the cold, yes. Eat fats. But how many people in the United States want to keep from losing weight?"

A more exact study of the effects of hot and cold weather on what we eat comes from the National Institute for Medical Research in London. There two scientists, Drs. O. G. Edholm and R. Goldsmith, summed up a series of studies of members of the British Antarctic Survey Team, and British soldiers in the hot, humid climate of Aden.

Some of the conclusions agreed with other researchers, but some did not. The amount of food we eat, the British researchers feel, is not influenced by the cold climate, although the men in the Antarctic gained eight times as much weight in a year as did the men back home. They would lose weight when they worked hard out of doors, or on long sledging expeditions, but they would gain it all back if allowed to eat whatever they pleased.

In hot weather—especially in hot, humid weather—hard work meant a pronounced weight loss, and it wasn't simply due to a loss of water. It may be that it was due to eating less in the heat. They found that given a free dietary hand, people ate one-quarter less food when the weather was hot than they did when it was temperate.

Logically, then, they suggested that people should eat more in hot climates if they must do heavy work. Yet hot climates tend to take appetites away. The soldiers in Aden, even when they did heavy work, ate less than they did back home. Their appetites seemed to be gone with the heat, and the reason, according to the British, may lie in skin temperature. They believe that low skin temperatures stimulate appetite, and high skin temperatures depress it.

Why this should be is still unknown, but there seems clear evidence that appetite is depressed by heat and stimulated by cold. But, then, so is the ability to work depressed by heat. Rising body temperature makes it difficult.

Cold weather causes us to put on weight; as if responding to some long-buried urge, we seem to want to get a padding of fat around us. It's a logical urge because, in the cold, the extra fat acts as insulation. The Eskimos have it almost as a racial characteristic. They tend to be short and stout and shaped to contain heat.

But today our civilization can provide outer garments that are as good insulation as that layer of fat, and can be shed very easily as well. They obviously cause no extra strain on the body. The extra fat we put on during the cold is not really necessary, if the London researchers are correct. They stress that we shouldn't eat more in the cold winter than we do in the hot summer.

But we are driven by some submerged urge to eat more when the temperature falls. The loaded holiday table represents protection against the oncoming winter. We equate the Thanksgiving turkey, candied sweets, mince pies, and puddings with the frozen cold of coming winter. We may be overfed, but we're ready to face the cold.

With the London study's results in mind, another group of researchers put some men under double stress from cold and diet. In cold weather, dressed inadequately, the men were given a diet low in calories and protein and made to do jobs requiring normal physical activity.

The men tried but after a day or two became incapable of working. It took them three days of normal eating to get back in shape.

A Diet to Beat the Heat

The need for water in hot weather has been mentioned before. Heat stress requires that a good deal of water be replaced, but cold stress does not. One reason the body needs water is that when we take in more proteins or minerals than we can metabolize, we must have additional water to flush them out. That's why a great deal of water should go with any diet high in protein.

In the summer, heat often makes us cut down on our protein intake. In general, heat takes away appetite; it often seems too much effort to eat. But too little protein in any weather can be a dangerous thing. This is particularly true of the woman in the early stages of pregnancy. There is evidence, presented earlier in the book, that a lack of protein in the early months of pregnancy may cause birth defects. The evidence is fragmentary, but should be considered. The tendency of dieters to cut down on protein in hot weather and to concentrate on salads and fruit is unwise.

Some fad diets suggest that high-protein foods—red meat, eggs, and cheese—speed up the metabolism and may make you feel the heat more than salads and fruit. The implication is to go off proteins when the weather gets hot. But this is really a time when we often need more protein in our diet. This is not only true for the pregnant woman, but for the average person as well.

Studies around the world have shown that in the tropics people tend to eat low-protein diets. The reasons are difficult to ascertain: They may be economic, or because protein is not available, or even for religious reasons. Whatever the cause, tropical people often live on predominantly vegetarian diets, high in carbohydrates, low in total calories, and deficient in most essential nutrients.

The result of such protein-poor diets show up in people of all ages, but especially in the children. This is tragic, but the people have very little choice. In most tropical countries proteins are simply not available. However, they are available in the United States, and it is something of a shock to find fad diets advising a low-protein summer diet.

Dos and Don'ts

Here are a few good rules about weather and food to keep in mind: (1) Eat enough protein in all seasons. (2) Replace the minerals lost through sweating in hot weather. (3) Salt your food well, but remember that fruit juices are also a good source of sodium and potassium. (4) Stay away from creamed foods in the heat. They are incubators of bacterial infection. (5) On the same note, thaw frozen foods in the refrigerator during the summer to prevent infections. Remember, the weather affects not only your body, but the food that goes into it.

An excellent diet that was developed recently works well in summer and winter. Low in fat, but high in protein and carbohydrates, it follows the suggestion given to me by Beverly Daniel and gets its carbohydrates not from sugars and starches, but from fruits and vegetables. Pioneered by Dr. Herman Tarnower of the Scarsdale, New York, Medical Group, and known as the "Scarsdale Diet," it seems to have taken the East Coast by storm. If followed exactly, it always takes off weight, sometimes as much as twenty pounds in two weeks.

It is basically a two-week diet, since it lacks certain necessary food elements: fats, yellow vegetables, and whole-grain cereals.

Breakfast is always the same: half a grapefruit, one slice of dry protein toast, and coffee or tea without milk or sugar. Lunches have a protein dish: cottage cheese, tuna fish or salmon, cold cuts, cheese combined with raw or cooked spinach or tomatoes. One or two lunches are all fruit salad, as much as you can eat.

Dinners consist of a wisely rotated selection of protein: fish, steak, lamb, eggs and cheese, chicken, steak. The second course is either vegetable or salad.

The diet allows no alcohol, salad dressing, or sugar. And because of its dietetic balance it fills you up as it takes the weight off.

Chapter Eighteen

What Weather Does for (and to) Sports

One summer when my children were in their early teens, my wife and I took our family across America on a "get-acquainted-with-your-country trip." We traveled west, stopping at national parks. At the Grand Canyon my children enviously watched the other tourists going toward the bottom of the canyon by burro and on foot.

"We're walking down," my eleven-year-old boy announced, and my thirteen-year-old daughter nodded. "We can do it easily. We'll be down and back for supper."

"You'll do nothing of the kind," my wife said firmly. "You have no idea of what a hike like that means."

"It's more than a mile down, and it's a brutal climb back up," I said. "There's no way we're going to let you do it, so forget it."

They tried to get us to change our minds, and later sneaked off and raced down the trail for a quarter of a mile. Then, realizing how late it was, they began climbing back as fast as they could. By the time they reached the top they could hardly stand. They were gasping for air and covered with sweat, their faces pale and drawn.

"We were so scared," they told us when they confessed what they had done. "Halfway up we were sure we'd never make it— we couldn't catch our breaths. But it was so easy going down!"

My oldest daughter looked at them with superior knowledge and said, "Dummies. It's always easier going down."

That was it, naturally. Going down involves no strain, and not much expenditure of energy. Breathing gets easier as you approach sea level, but coming back up a steep climb like that must be done slowly. The air is thinner and you must adapt.

Later, the park ranger stationed at the rim told me that quite a few tourists who had started out to walk the trail both ways had to be brought back by burro. "The trouble in climbing up from the bottom is that it's an eight-hour hike, and some of the people who try it just keep right on going. They gasp and wheeze and don't pay any attention to what their body is saying until they collapse. And yet I've seen guys out of condition take the climb back in easy stages, resting every hundred feet, and they make it with no serious problems."

Many years later I remembered what the ranger said when I walked down to the bottom of Bryce Canyon, in Utah. I had been so enthralled by the "Martian landscape" formations that I felt I had to get down among them. I climbed down out of the hot, dry air above to wander through greenery, water, and the cool shade of the towering red carvings.

I went back up slowly, and I paused every hundred feet to take my pulse. It raced furiously. I'd wait until it came back to a fast 130 beats, then I'd climb again. By checking my pulse all the way up and never letting it get above 130, I made the climb with no physical inconvenience.

How to Handle Weather Stress

"The trick," a physiologist told me when I described this experience, "is to adapt. Always it's adaptation, in walking, in sports, in any exercise—let your body adapt. That's one way to handle the stress of weather."

"But that climb up, is that weather adaptation?"

"Of course. Altitude, high and low pressure, the heat of the sun, the stress on your body from that heat—it's all weather. Your body adapted to the climb just as you adapt to any weather change."

I was reminded of my visit to the laboratory at the Pierce Foundation at Yale. There I had seen men going through different forms of exercise while Dr. Stolwijk studied their reactions. "What we're after is adaptation," he had told me. "How does the body's heating and cooling system react to exercise? It's no accident that the athletic type, the person who enjoys skiing in the winter, also likes to run or play tennis in the summer. He has learned to adapt to all different weather patterns. You could say he is a man for all seasons."

"You mean he's active all the time?"

"I mean that he knows how to pace his activities. He knows when to keep going and when to stop. He's attuned to his own body."

"I think of an athlete as someone who's in such good condition that he can outlast the average man," I said doubtfully.

"Yes, he can, but he also knows when to stop. He listens when the heat or cold says, 'Slow down!' The body must stay at a constant temperature, at about ninety-nine degrees. When you overexert and build up too much heat, your body tries to adapt by cooling you. If you're too cold, the body conserves heat by sending blood to your head and trunk, keeping it away from the legs and arms, where it loses its heat."

"But doesn't that affect your circulation?" I asked.

"If you're an athlete or if you're in good physical condition, it won't. Your circulation will be good enough to keep some blood coursing through the capillaries of your hands and feet. You won't get leg cramps or numb fingers and toes. If you're not in condition, you will.

"In the heat your body sends blood to the skin's surface where the evaporation of sweat can cool it. That's why sweating is so important in sports, especially if you're exercising in the summer. If you can't evaporate your sweat, the heat builds up and you get symptoms of heat stress: a flushed face, faintness, swelling in your hands and feet. These are all warning signals. The body is saying, 'For God's sake, cool me off!' And you'd better listen."

The athlete, or even the average person who likes sports, I began to realize, should be aware of the weather if it can have such powerful effects. There must be any number of cautions and conditions that apply to sports—professional and amateur.

I called an orthopedic surgeon who is involved with sports medicine and asked him to give me some time.

"I could, but there isn't much I could tell you," he said. "I know a few obvious things, but there has really been little work done in this field. Let me give you the name of a friend who might help you out."

The "friend" was affiliated with an institute for sports medicine. He, too, drew a blank. "I don't know of anyone who knows that much about weather affecting the athlete," he told me, "although I certainly think it should be considered. Let me give you a name of a friend. . . ."

So it went from friend to friend. Everyone I spoke to was involved in one aspect or another of physical training and athletics, but none was an expert on the effect of weather on the athlete's health.

In the end I had to fall back on the biometeorologists to gather some basic information. And that's what it was—basic. This is an important but neglected field that needs to be explored, if I can trust the opinion of all those sports-oriented persons to whom I spoke.

One man, a football coach for a small southern college, said, "I know how important it is. I see all kinds of problems because my boys are out in the wrong weather. But it's only by trial and error that I've learned a little about what to do and what not to do. There are no published guidelines."

And this from an Australian track coach: "In our country, in the tropical part of it, we have a few rules. For instance, we don't hold three-mile races because it is so hard for the body to get rid of the excess heat it can build up in fifteen minutes. You run a race in eighty-two-degree heat and your men will perform as much as one-third less well than guys in the temperate parts of the country. They'll just be that much slower. Oh, we give them some salt and water, and they do a little better, and if we do make a mistake and hold an event in really hot weather, these guys have a painful recovery, really painful."

How Climate Affects Performance

While on the trail of the knowledgeable weather-oriented sportsman, I met a physician who had attended the 1968 Olympic Games in Mexico City. He was an enthusiastic sports fan and an athlete himself.

"Those games were fascinating to me," he said, "and Mexico City's climate was one reason. I know all about the problems that athletes from high altitudes face when they come down to sea level—like the soccer players from Peru. They have a hard time, as do the sea-level guys who go up in the mountains to play. But those Olympic Games were held in middle altitudes. Mexico City is high on a plateau, but not high enough to be dangerous. I wanted to see what would happen to athletes from sea level when they competed up on that plateau."

"What did you find out?"

"One curious thing. In a general, overall way, at this altitude, the performances of the gold-medal winners, men and women, were better for short distances than they had been at sea level."

"Why do you specify short distances?" I asked.

"Because for long distances, their records at lower altitudes were better. Now I can understand that. What I cannot understand is why they should do better in the short distances. As a matter of fact, the running speed at Mexico City was so fast that all the finalists in the hurdles had actually to shorten their strides, to keep from running into each other."

"Surely there has to be a reason," I said.

"The reason is the altitude. If you asked me why, I would have to guess. Altitude has an effect on how fast we breathe. Maybe they breathed in too fast at first, taking in more oxygen than they needed, and sort of priming their metabolism. But that's only a guess."

"Were there any other weather factors that could influence them?"

"Well, temperature of course. The optimal temperature for sprinting and jumping is around fifty to fifty-four degrees, and for distance events between fifty-seven and seventy-five degrees. In Mexico City it was somewhere about forty-five degrees, give or take a few degrees.

"Was there anything else that could have interfered with their performance?"

He shook his head. "Weatherwise? Not that I know of. I know that shouting crowds can help track performers do better, just the way silent crowds can help golfers. I guess those are factors, too. But I don't think they mattered in Mexico City during the Olympics. Temperature, maybe. Altitude, certainly. But don't pin me down as to why. I just don't know."

A man who could be pinned down as to "why" was Dr. Gerhardt Hentschel of the German Democratic Republic. Dr. Hentschel is director of a research institute devoted to bio-meteorology. "Under certain circumstances," he said, "some decrease of atmospheric pressure may be desirable." This was the situation at Mexico City during the 1968 Olympics.

Dr. Hentschel suggests that when athletes do get to altitudes this high, there are changes in their carbon dioxide balance which increase their number of red blood cells. They then have a built-in advantage over performers in the lowlands. They will be able to use the oxygen they get more efficiently, and they will then require less strength to run a brief distance. If they use their full strength for the same distance, their performance will improve. But the advantage will not hold up over long distances.

Dr. Hentschel suggests that when it comes to adjusting to new weather patterns, the trained athlete is better than the untrained person, but even his ability to adapt runs down toward the end of a competitive event.

The greatest upset comes when we send athletes from one hemisphere to another. There is not only the burden of coming from winter to summer or summer to winter, the stress of excess heat or cold, but sometimes there is also the problem of an upset to their day and night habits. It's an aggravated form of jet lag.

To really perform at top condition for any sustained time, the athlete should get to the new area, new climate, and new weather pattern two or three weeks before the event takes place. This would give him time enough to adjust, and he would be in tip-top shape.

It is not likely that we would send our athletes so far in advance to the nation in which the Olympic Games are being held. We're usually too busy training them at home. And there's another consideration in connection with adaptation. Sending the athletes in advance wouldn't always work. If the athlete is going to a warm, moist climate he is going to be under considerable strain and it would be best for him to spend very little time there before the event; the problem of adaptation gives way to the problem of weather.

For Sunday Athletes Only

Dr. Hentschel has studied the problem of weather and sports in more detail than our own sports-oriented physicians—although in the United States we do have an Institute of Sports Medicine. Most of this institute's concern, however, is with the physical condition of the athlete, not his performance under different weather conditions. Dr. Hentschel and his associates in the German Democratic Republic, attuned to biometeorology as they are, are much more concerned with climatic stress.

"Stress," Dr. Hentschel emphasizes, "always varies with the sport. In running, especially marathon running, heat metabolism and oxygen supply are decisive." He also believes that the Sunday athlete—the untrained runner or tennis player, jogger, or cyclist, is more sensitive to the weather than the trained professional athlete.

Dr. Hentschel cautions the Sunday athlete that hot, muggy weather slows down the evaporation of sweat, and that it may be impossible for him to dissipate body heat fast enough. A wind, even a light one, can overcome some of the dangers of mugginess. It increases the evaporation of sweat and helps cool the body.

A sweatshirt naturally increases sweating but will not permit maximum evaporation. The sweat will roll off in drops, and sweat that forms droplets doesn't cool. The best cooling sweat is the thin all-over kind.

During sustained exertion, such as a marathon or a long tennis match, we may lose, Dr. Hentschel says, almost four quarts of liquid in an hour. And not only must this liquid be replenished; lost body salts must also be replaced.

If the exercise takes place on a hot, dry day, we may gain more heat from the sun than we lose by sweating. The result can be heat exhaustion.

The best weather for the Sunday athlete is the fresh, cool,

clean air found after the passing of a cold front. It is generally stimulating, physically and psychologically, and makes for best performance.

One of the most important problems facing the Sunday athlete is pollution. The weather pattern called a Bermuda high—an anticyclonic area of high barometric pressure—can spread over the Northeast and bring with it relentlessly hot, humid, and pollution-filled air. In the spring of 1978 the temperature hovered at 93° and the THI at 83 day after day.

The Massachusetts State Department of Environmental Protection gave its usual warning to elderly people and to those with heart or respiratory ailments to take it easy. But in an unusual warning they also cautioned "physical-fitness buffs" against exercise. This recognition of the danger of exercise during pollution alerts is encouraging. We tend to forget how dangerous pollution can be. Dr. Hentschel found that when the air is polluted, humans instinctively compensate by taking shallow breaths, unconsciously trying to keep the pollutants from their lungs. The athlete, however, is caught in a dilemma. He must breathe deeply to get enough oxygen, and with the oxygen he will take in a greater amount of pollution than his sedentary brother, and do a greater amount of damage to his entire body. This then is a time when exercise, far from being a help, can become a danger.

This danger is so real that Dr. Hentschel has laid down guidelines for the placement of outdoor sports stadiums upwind from polluting industry. If the winds are varied, he says, the stadium should be built somewhere else.

Many states have ignored such guidelines, if indeed they

knew they existed. New York and New Jersey, for example, have put their outdoor stadiums near centers of industrial pollution and close to enormous airports with a constant outpouring of pollutants.

Dos and Don'ts

A summing up of biometeorological advice for Sunday athletes—the sometime jogger, tennis player, golfer, and even gardener—includes a number of dos and don'ts. The ideal outdoor exercise temperature is between 40° and 60°, although lower and higher temperatures should not prevent you from exercising. It is only when the temperature gets up as high as 80° or 85°, and you cannot readily lose your body heat, that you must desist. And, of course, humidity is a factor. The lower the humidity, the higher the temperature you can stand.

Plan your exercise for the early morning or the late afternoon. Avoid the heat of midday. In winter, remember the wind-chill factor. It may be colder than the thermometer registers.

In the winter, cover your hands with mittens. If the air is bitter, try a face mask. Some cardiac patients who jog have designed face masks with breathing tubes going into their shirts. The air they draw into their lungs is then warmed by the body. Not only do they not irritate their lungs and shock their systems, but they cut down on the heat loss from their bodies.

In cold weather, be sure your chest is warm. This will protect your heart from cold stress. Wear thermal underwear under your jogging suit.

In the summer, dress loosely. If it's warm enough, run bare-chested if you are a man and with a skimpy top if you are a woman. Let the sweat cool you.

If you run in the rain, the only real danger is the slippery road.

Always take the wind into account. Apart from the wind-chill factor, running into the wind is bad for you in any sport, and running into a strong wind is downright dangerous. It interferes with your breathing.

In the summer heat, be sure to drink enough water. Two glasses before you start your tennis game or morning jog and two glasses afterwards is a good rule, and you would do well to add a pinch of salt to each glass of water.

Don't run in a nylon shirt. Cotton is best, but if you must wear an artificial fiber, be sure the weave is open.

If you must exercise in the heat, cut your exercise down. Forgo that extra set of tennis or the last time around the track. Limit your golf to nine holes, and, in any case, adapt. Build up slowly to your best level of performance in either hot or cold weather.

Chapter Nineteen

How to Enjoy a
Weather-wise Vacation

Very few things are as disappointing as selecting a vacation spot and finding, once you get there, that the weather is miserable. The only thing worse is to get to a vacation spot and find something about the weather that troubles you and no one else. You may be sensitive to the altitude, the wind, the humidity and temperature, or even the changing fronts.

There should be a set of weather-sensitivity guidelines for hotels, resorts, and campgrounds. The nature of these guidelines is suggested in the work of Dr. André Cornet, associate professor of hydrology and climatology at the University of Paris Faculty of Medicine.

In a discussion of European health resorts, Dr. Cornet notes that most of them were chosen empirically. The people who started going found that they were helped. Somehow the climate in at least some of the spas seemed to make them feel better. What is true for these health resorts is also true for vacation areas, and we can use Dr. Cornet's analysis of places best for weather sensitives to help us choose our own vacation spot.

The first requisite, according to Dr. Cornet, is a comfortable temperature range without much fluctuation. This minimizes the load on the heat-regulating system of the body. Since hot or cold winds and fronts stress the body, the perfect location should be free of these. The THI should remain close to 50 percent and the temperature should be whatever you find comfortable.

Dr. Cornet suggests that valleys, being soothing, are best for people in need of calm and rest. People suffering from insomnia, anxiety, high blood pressure, or respiratory difficulties should look for valley resorts no higher than 900 feet, with little rain, and enough sunshine and plenty of good, green forest. Valleys like this are usually stable in climate, protected from the ups and downs of barometric pressure. At a vacation resort in such a place "the heart slows down, the nervous system becomes calm, and regular sleep is restored," Dr. Cornet assures us.

One thing to watch for in this idyllic climate is any allergic irritation. Find out when the pollen season ends and go only then.

If you haven't got insomnia, rheumatic aches or pains, anxieties, bouts of the blues, or cardiac problems, then you may not need the peaceful valley. You might want to choose a mountain slope as the ideal body recharger. Dr. Cornet recommends a sunny slope, about 6,000 feet up, where the humidity is half what it is at sea level. He stresses the purity of mountain air and, if you need it, the benefit of the additional ultraviolet radiation you get that high. The slightly lower air pressure and oxygen content have a good effect on our lungs. We take deep breaths and clear out all the stagnant corners.

The people that benefit most from mountain resorts are those who are overworked physically and mentally but otherwise in good health. If you are getting over an illness or have a touch of asthma, mountains are good for you.

Forests, whether in the valley or on mountain slopes, are

calming places and, according to Dr. Cornet, have "remarkably stable electric fields." This would produce a constant negative-ion balance, a healthy effect, and it may be why so many of us feel an almost religious sense of calm in the quiet of a large forest.

If valleys bore you and mountains are out of your reach, try a lake. Lakes tend to be heat stable. The temperature of the water doesn't vary as much as the air does, and it cools the air on warm days and warms it on cool ones. The ocean, too, has this same equalizing effect, and the seashore has always been a favorite vacationing spot. In terms of health, the salt breeze is supposed to be good for almost any illness. It is certainly rich in iodine and iodine is good for the thyroid. And it is low in allergens. The inshore breezes clear pollen and pollutants out of the air.

How the Ocean Affects Metabolism

According to many physicians, the air near the ocean gives a gentle lift to body metabolism. Studies of people who vacation at the seashore show that their red-blood-cell count increases. This, it is believed, is part of general body stimulation. Seawater itself, in the view of European biometeorologists, has a beneficial effect on the body. Bathing in it increases appetite by causing blood to move from the surface vessels to deeper ones, thereby stimulating the intestinal system. It also has a desirable effect on the parasympathetic system, and somehow the salt spray, or water itself, cuts down the number of harmful bacteria in the mouth and nose.

The climate at the seashore has always been considered healthful, and in Europe *thalassotherapy*, the use of seawater and sea climate to overcome health problems, is generally accepted as useful. Claims for thalassotherapy run from some modest proposals to a sort of catchall panacea for respiratory disease, skin problems, diabetes, heart disease, anemia, and a host of psychological ills.

How much is enthusiasm and how much solid fact is hard to decide. Psychologically the seashore may indeed help. We feel cleansed somehow, uplifted and excited by the breaking surf. We are all children of the sea, in a way, since all life originated there. Perhaps coming back to it makes us feel young again, brings us closer to our source.

A final word on resorts and vacation places. In Europe there are a number of spas where the soil or the water is hailed as the healing factor. Some are so popular that their mineral waters are bottled and exported to other countries. We have our own mineral springs in America—places like Saratoga, New York, where the spring water is so foul-tasting it just "has to be healthy."

The waters at these mineral springs are not connected with the weather, but in some locations electrical charges in the ground may saturate the low-lying air. We may be basking in an excess of negative ions similar to those found in forests, or absorbing low levels of radiation from the mud and rock. In either case, there seems to be some benefit from these spas with their mud baths, sand baths, and hot mineral waters to drink and bathe in.

In the light of this, it would be interesting to examine our own areas of unusual earth activity, places like Yellowstone Park with its geysers and bubbling mudholes. Is there any benefit in the Yellowstone mud for arthritis or other illnesses? If we bottled Old Faithful, would we have a cure for diabetes?

Choosing the Best City for Your Vacation

It's all well and good to set guidelines for the perfect vacation spot, weatherwise, in mountains, valleys, lakes, and seashore. But some people flock to cities for fun. After all, the cities have all the cultural and much of the historical excitement. How many families visit Washington, D.C., every year to see how our government works? How many honeymooners ride the cable cars in San Francisco? How many drive around Beverly Hills, looking for elusive stars, or come to New York for a taste of the Big Apple?

Like my friend Gladys, they may be in for a severe shock. She had always wanted to go to New Orleans. Finally, one lovely June, she got her chance. Sadly enough, June was lovely only back in Duluth. In New Orleans it was God-awful, the worst heat that Gladys had ever endured. It never occurred to her to check the weather first. If she had, she would have discovered that October was the ideal month to visit New Orleans.

If you know ahead of time what the weather is in a city, then you are better able to decide whether or not you can take the weather—and this decision must be based on your own weather sensitivity. For Gladys, hot, humid weather was disastrous.

The obvious problem is that almost all of us are restricted in our vacation times. We are usually limited to the summer months and while many of us can pick the time of summer we want, for most of us vacation time is determined by somebody else's work schedule as well as by our own. And yet, for just about every month in the year, there are sunny, comfortable cities to visit in our country.

As a guide to the unwary weather-sensitive traveler, I have prepared a weather-sensitivity chart of all the major vacation cities in the United States, along with the best month for visiting them and the weather you'll find there. Weather sensitivity being what it is, however, one man's comfort is another man's ache. I've selected a group of typical weather patterns that include most ideal climates. The best in my opinion, is plenty of sunshine and comfortable temperatures, but some will want to forgo the sunshine, and others will be content with intermittent sun so long as the air is pleasant and cool.

The chart lists five different weather patterns, during different months in different cities. I've based my chart on Dr.

Harflinger's biometeorological studies of the climate in the United States.

The chart is based on the average weather in each city during each month, but weather is variable and you can never be certain that it will live up to the average. You always take a chance with it, but with this chart the risks are lessened.

Yes, We Can Change the Weather

In this book I have sketched the effects of the planet's weather on health, but there are other kinds of weather—the local climates of certain cities and even the microclimates within our homes, office, and factories—that affect health. These microweathers can be controlled if we put effort and research into it.

The downtown areas of our cities tend to be vast spreads of steel, glass, and concrete, which reduce evaporation but allow the runoff of rainwater to be complete.

Cities can change wind patterns. Tall buildings stop some winds, and others are channeled through city canyons as they are through natural valleys. Every large city is an island of heat held by its concrete all day and radiated out at night—and of course the air above and within most of our cities is polluted.

We can change these microclimates so that they are more pleasant, more in accord with our weather sensitivity. We can plant trees, build parks, create open spaces, and employ different building materials. Reflective and absorbant paint and panels would change the heat balance of the city. Using mass transit systems instead of private cars and controlling industrial pollution would improve the environment.

But one thing we can do right now is control the weather in our own homes. We can control the cold with central heating and the heat and humidity with air conditioning and fans, and even purify our air with electronic filters.

Major Vacation Cities	Plenty of Sunshine, Comfortable Temperatures	Plenty of Sunshine, Some Heat	Plenty of Sunshine, Cool Air	Half Sun and Half Clouds, Comfortable Temperatures	Mostly Cloudy and Cool
ATLANTA	Oct, Nov			Mar, Apr	Jan, Dec
BOSTON	June, July, Aug		Sept	May	Jan, Nov, Dec
CHARLESTON	Mar, Apr, Oct, Nov		Dec		
CHICAGO		July, Aug, Sept		May	Jan, Feb, Nov, Dec
COLUMBUS	May, Sept	Aug		Apr	Jan, Feb, Mar, Dec
DALLAS	Nov, Oct			Feb, Mar	Jan
DENVER	May, June, July, Aug, Sept		Jan, Feb, Mar, Apr, Oct, Nov, Dec		
DULUTH	July, Aug			June, Sept	Jan, Oct, Nov, Dec
LAS VEGAS	Apr, May, June July, Aug, Sept		Jan, Feb, Mar, Oct, Nov, Dec		
LOS ANGELES	Jan, Feb, Mar, Apr, Oct, Nov, Dec	May, June, July, Aug, Sept			
MIAMI BEACH		Jan, Feb, Dec			
MINNEAPOLIS	Sept	Aug	Oct		Jan, Nov, Dec

Major Vacation Cities	Plenty of Sunshine, Comfortable Temperatures	Plenty of Sunshine, Some Heat	Plenty of Sunshine, Cool Air	Half Sun and Half Clouds, Comfortable Temperatures	Mostly Cloudy and Cool
NASHVILLE	Oct			Mar, Apr	Jan, Feb, Dec
NEW ORLEANS	Nov	Sept		Feb, Mar	
NEW YORK	Sept	June, July, Aug		May	Jan, Dec
PHILADELPHIA				Apr, May, Sept	Jan, Dec
PHOENIX	Jan, Feb, Mar, Apr, Oct, Nov, Dec	May, June			
ST. LOUIS	May, Oct	Sept		Apr	Jan, Feb, Dec
SALT LAKE CITY	May, June, July, Aug, Sept		Apr, Oct		Jan, Dec
SAN FRANCISCO	Feb, Mar, Apr, May, June, July, Aug, Sept, Oct, Nov			Jan, Dec	
SEATTLE	July			May, June, Aug, Sept	Jan, Feb, Mar, Apr, Oct, Nov, Dec
TAMPA	Jan	Feb, Mar, Dec			
WASHINGTON, D.C.				Apr, Sept, Oct	Dec

In the future we may even control the air pressure in the homes and perhaps in the cities. Weather domes on the model of Houston's Astrodome have been suggested to enclose entire cities.

Some scientists predict that some day man will totally manage the entire planet's weather. With the vast power available from nuclear fusion, if and when we master it, we may be able to change the earth's surface. If we ever learn to make artificial clouds we could block sunlight at will. This would let us change the radiation balance between the sun and the earth, cooling great areas of sun-baked desert and perhaps turning them into forest or farmland.

By altering the way the earth reflects light, we might control evaporation in the oceans and lakes. Reforesting areas that have been stripped bare would reduce flood damage and equalize temperatures. Covering some of the polar ice with black dust, as sad as it might be esthetically, would trap the sun's heat and melt the ice. This might make the polar regions livable. We would need other devices to keep the melted snow and ice from refreezing, but those too would be possible with the unlimited power given us by nuclear fusion.

Certain alcohols on water become monomolecular films that prevent evaporation. We could keep lakes and rivers from evaporating by covering them with such films, which would interfere with the natural cycle of water and rain. Seeding the clouds with solid carbon dioxide to produce rain is another way of breaking the cycle, and by towing icebergs from the Arctic and the Antarctic we might even be able to supply the arid parts of our world with vast reservoirs of fresh water. (A pilot proposal to tow an iceberg to Saudi Arabia to provide drinking water is under active consideration in 1978.)

Even though these methods might not convert deserts to gardens, they might, along with irrigation, go a long way toward making deserts livable.

These methods are speculative, far out, and perhaps dangerous, but some weather manipulation is practical and inevitable.

A federal panel supports this concept and sees weather modification possible by the 1980s. "In the early nineteen eighties we will probably be able to increase accumulations of mountain snow by ten to thirty percent, and before the end of that decade achieve similar increases in rainfall on Middle Western farms." So says the Weather Modification Advisory Board, reporting on the national weather modification plan of 1976. It may run into the hundreds of millions of dollars to get the program off the ground.

If the government is willing to spend this much money on weather modification, surely it should consider using some lesser sum to fund a program that would deal with health and its relationship to weather. My modest proposal for a "People's Weather Service," suggested earlier in this book, is a good first step in that direction.

With such a service, doctors, meteorologists, and biometeorologists could begin to collect significant data about weather sensitivity and its impact not only on individual health but on the health of the nation.

Selected References

Austin, H. M., Ambulance Weather, *Climate and Health, NOAA Reprint* 6:4, October 1976.

Barnea, M., Influence of Atmospheric Factors on Cerebral Vascular Accident Mortality, *Rev. Med. Intern.* 21:47, January-March 1976.

Bartko, D., et al., Biometeorological Study of the Focal Brain Ischemia, *Cesk. Neurol. Neurochir.* 38:274, September 1975.

Becker, R. O., Electromagnetic Forces and Life Forces, *Technology Review*, Cambridge, Mass., MIT, 1972.

Beregszaszi, G., et al., Relationship Between Asthmatic Bronchitis and Some Meteorological Factors, *Z. Kinderheilkd.* 117:223, 1974.

Bernett, P., et al., Relationship Between Sport Injuries and Weather, *Fortschr. Med.* 93:99, January 1975.

Blum, H. F., *Carcinogenesis by Ultraviolet Light*, Princeton, N.J.: Princeton University Press, 1959.

Brezowsky, H., and Kastner, M., Wettervorgänge als Auslosender Faktor des Akuten Glaukomanfalls, *Med. Monatschr.* 8:538, 1958.

Burch, G. E., *Hot Climates, Man and His Heart*, Springfield, Ill.: C. C. Thomas, 1962.

Carlson, L. D., Human Tolerance to Cold, *J. Occupat. Med.* 2:129, 1960.

———, et al., Adaptive Changes During Exposure to Cold, *J. Appl. Physiol.* 5:672, 1953.

Danon, A., et al., Effects of Hot Dry Desert Winds on Man, *Biometeorology, Supp. Int. J. Biomet.* 4:71, 1969.

———, Mechanisms of Reaction to Heat Stress, *Int. J. Biomet.* 13:95, 1969.

Dingle, A. N., Pollen Counts and the Hayfever Problem, *Science* 117:3029, 1953.

Driscoll, D. M., Weather Influences on Mortality and Morbidity, *Rev. Environ. Health* 1:283, 1974.

Dubs, R., et al., Meteorological Observations Concerning Hemorrhages After Tonsillectomy, *Laryngol. Rhinol. Otol.* 54:755, 1975.

Ellis, F. P., et al., Mortality During Heat Waves in New York City, July 1972 and August 1973, *Environ. Res.* 10:1, 1975.

Eriksson, E., Composition of Atmospheric Pollution, *Tellus* 4:215, 1954.

Faust, V. *Biometeorologie*, Stuttgart: Hippokrates Verlag, 1978.

———, *Wetterfühligkeit*, Munich: Mosaik Verlag, 1977.

———, What Is Weather Sensitivity? *ZFA* 52:225, February 1976.

———, Psychophysiologic Reactions to Meteorologic Influences, *ZFA* 52:237, February 1976.

Fleck, H., *Inrtoduction to Nutrition*, New York: Macmillan, 1971.

Folk, G. E., *Introduction to Environmental Physiology*, Philadelphia: Lea & Feibiger, 1966.

Forsdyke, A. G., *Weather and Weather Forecasting*, New York: Bantam, 1971.

Frank, B. S., *Dr. Frank"s No-Aging Diet*, New York: Dial Press, 1976.

Geller, S. H., et al., The Moon, Weather and Mental Hospital Contacts, *J. Psychiatr. Nurs.* 14:13, January 1976.

Givoni, B. Architectural and Urban Planning in Relation to Weather and Climate, *Prog. Biomet.* 1:183, 1974.

Gold, G., Development of Heat Pyrexia, *JAMA* 173:1175, 1960.

Gostynski, M., et al., Meteorotropic Activity of the Weather Conditions, and Their Role in Suicide Epidemiology, *Zentralbl. Bakteriol.* 161:158, October 1975.

Griffiths, J. F., *Applied Climatology*, London: Oxford University Press, 1966.

Grob, P. R., et al., The Effect of Weather on Some Infectious Diseases, *J. Roy. Coll. Gen. Prac.* 25:158, April 1975.

Gualtierotti, R., et al., *Bioclimatology, Biometeorology and Aeroionotherapy*, Milan: Carlo Erba Foundation, 1968.

Guaquelin, M., *How Atmospheric Conditions Affect Your Health,* New York: Stein & Day, 1971.

———, *L'Hérédité Plantetaire*, Paris: Planète, 1966.

Harflinger, O., Bioklimatologie der Vereinigten Staaten von Amerika, *Notabene Medici* 7:46, May 1977.

Harsh, G. F., The Correlation Between Humidity and House Dust Sensitivity, *First Int. Congr. for Aller., Basel* 118, 1951.

Hatsell, C. P., A Note on Jogging on a Windy Day, *Trans. Biomed. Eng.* 22:428, September 1975.

Hollander, J. L., Environment and Musculoskeletal Diseases, *Arch. Environ. Health* 6:527, April 1963.

Houston, C. S., Some Observations on Acclimatization to High Altitudes, *New Eng. J. Med.* 253:964, 1955.

Iurik, O. E., et al., Effect of Meteorologic Factors on Patients with Hypothalamic Disorders, *Vrach. Delo.* 6:116, June 1974.

Jokl, E., and Jokl, P., *Exercise and Altitude*, Basel: Karger, 1968.

Jungmann, H., Human Response to Meteorological Stress as a Function of Age, *Prog. Biometeorol.* 1:285, 1974.

Kerdo, I., et al., *New Possibilities in the Increasing of Driving Safety*, Budapest: Medicor, 1973.

Knobloch, H., and Pasamanick, B., Seasonal Variations in Complications of Pregnancy, *Obstet. Gynec.* 12:110, 1958.

Kreider, M. B., et al., Effect of Continuous Cold Exposure on Nocturnal Body Temperature of Man, *J. Appl. Physiol.* 14:43, 1959.

Krueger, A. P., Are Air Ions Biologically Significant? *Int. J. Biomet.* 1972.

———, Are Negative Air Ions Good for You? *The New Scientist (United Kingdom)*, June 14, 1973.

Landsberg, H. E., Assessment of Human Bioclimate, *World Mete-*

orological Organization, Technical Note BN 690, 1971.

————, Biometeorological Aspects of Urban Climate, *Institute for Fluid Dynamics and Applied Mathematics, Technical Note BN 620,* September 1969.

————, *Weather and Health,* Garden City, N.Y.: Doubleday, 1969.

————, and Tromp, S. W., Proceedings of Seventh International Biometeorological Congress, *Int. J. Biomet.* 1975.

Lee, D. H., Biometeorological Consequences of Environmental Controls, *Environ. Health Prospect* 10:183, April 1975.

Licht, S., *Medical Climatology,* Baltimore, Maryland: Waverly Press, 1964.

Lidwell, O.M.A., and Lowbury, E. J., The Survival of Bacteria in Dust, II: The Effect of Atmospheric Humidity on the Survival of Bacteria, *J. Hygiene* 48:21, 1950.

Lind, A. R., The Optimal Exposure Time for the Development of Acclimatization to Heat, *Fed. Proc.* 22:704, 1963.

Mackie, B. S., and McGovern, V. J., The Mechanism of Solar Carcinogenesis, *AMA Arch. Derm.* 78:218, 1958.

Madaras, K., et al., The Effect of Weather Fronts on the Development of Periostitis of Dental Origin, *Fogorv. Sz.* 67:366, December 1974.

Magnuson, M. D., Relationship Between Precipitation and Traffic Accidents in Seattle, Washington, *Weekly Weather Crop Bull.* 16:46, 1957.

Malinskii, D. M., et al., Correlation Between Meteorological Factors and the Respiratory Morbidity in Organized Collectives under the Conditions of the Polar Regions, *Gig. Sanit.* 11:83, November 1974.

Neutra, R., Meteorological Factors and Eclampsia, *J. Obstet. Gynaecol. Br. Commonw.* 81:833, November 1974.

Neuwirth, R., et al., Weather-Climate-City, *ZFA* 52:243, February 1976.

Peacock, J. B., et al., Reported Morbidity and the Weather, *J. Roy. Coll. Gen. Pract.* 25:247, April 1975.

Persinger, M. A., Lag Responses in Mood Reports to Changes in the Weather Matrix, *Int. J. Biomet.* 19:108, June 1975.

Petterssen, S., *Introduction to Meteorology,* 3d ed., McGraw-Hill, New York, 1969.

Piccardi, G., *The Chemical Basis of Medical Climatology*, Spring-field, Ill.: C. C. Thomas, 1963.

Prindle, R. A., Notes Made During the London Fog in December, 1962, *Arch. Environ. Health* 7:493, 1963.

Priscu, R., et al., Meteorological Influences in Respiratory Diseases in Children, *Pediatria* 32:113, March-April 1974.

Rancht-Froemsdorff, W., The Diagnosis of "Weather Sensitivity" and "Weather Pain," *ZFA* 52:228, February 1976.

Reiter, R., Behavior of Atmospheric Electric Magnitudes at Seven Mountain Stations, *Technical Report, I, II, AF* 61:514, 1958.

Robinson, C. H., *Normal and Therapeutic Nutrition*, New York: Macmillan, 1972.

Rogot, E., Associations Between Coronary Mortality and the Weather, Chicago, 1967, *Public Health Report* 89:330, July-August 1974.

———, et al., Associations of Coronary and Stroke Mortality with Temperature and Snowfall in Selected Areas of the United States, 1962–1966, *Am. J. Epidemiol.* 103:656, June 1976.

Sauvage Nolting, W.J.J. De, Verband Tussen Geboortemaand en Schizophrenie en Manisch-depressieve Geestesziekten, *Ned. Tijdschr. Geneesk.* 95:3855, 1951.

Selby, M., and Selby, E., Beware the Witch's Wind, *National Wildlife Magazine*, August-September 1972.

Slonin, N. B., *Environmental Physiology*, St. Louis: C. V. Mosby, 1974.

Steer, R. G., Asthma and the Weather, *Med. J. Aust.* 1:38, January 1976.

Sulman, F. G., *Health, Weather and Climate*, Basel: Karger, 1976.

———, et al., Air Ionometry of Hot, Dry, Desert Winds (Sharav) and Treatment with Air Ions of Weather Sensitive Subjects, *Int. J. Biomet.* 18:313, 1974.

———, et al., Effect of Hot, Dry, Desert Winds on the Metabolism of Hormones and Minerals, *Proc. Lucknow Symp. on Arid Zones, UNESCO* 89, 1964.

Takahashi, Y., et al., Relationship Between Absence of Primary School Children and Meteorological Factors, *Jpn. J. Hyg.* 30:257, April 1975.

Taylor, C. F., *Elementary Meteorology*, Englewood Cliffs, N.J.: Prentice-Hall, 1954.

Tromp, S. W., *Medical Biometeorology*, New York: Elsevier, 1963.

————, The Possible Effects of Meteorological Stress on Cancer and Its Importance for Psychosomatic Cancer Research, *Experientia* 30: 1474, December 1974.

Wiehe, W. H., *The Physiological Effects of High Altitudes*, Oxford: Pergamon Press, 1964.

World Meteorological Organization, *A Survey of Human Biometeorology, Technical Note* 65, 1974.

Zhiznevskaia, E. M., Effect of Atmospheric Phenomena on the Course of Glaucoma, *Vestn. Oftalmol.* 3:28, May-June 1975.